Alice Taylor

a Country Miscellany

MOUNT
EAGLE

First published in 1998 by
Mount Eagle Publications Ltd.,
Dingle, Co. Kerry, Ireland

Text © Alice Taylor 1998

Photographs © Richard T. Mills 1998

The author has asserted her moral rights.

ISBN 1 902011 08 2

"The Cottage" was first published in Irish Cottages by Walter
Pfeiffer and Maura Shaffrey (Weidenfeld & Nicolson, 1990);
"Green Fields" is based on the Introduction by Alice Taylor to
the paperback edition of Green Fields by Stephen Rynne
(Brandon 1995); "The Women of Shawls" and "The Other Side
of the Brain" were first published in the Irish Independent; "A
Woman with a Mission" was first published in The Irish Times.

Typesetting by Red Barn Publishing, Skeagh, Skibbereen

Cover design by the Public Communications Centre, Dublin

Printed in Singapore

Contents

The Cottage	7
The Hatching House	14
Green Fields	19
Rural Reading	24
A Woman with a Mission	28
The Women of Shawls	32
Christmas in the Village Shop	37
The Forge	41
Something to Crow About	46
Herself Upstairs	50
What Have We Done to Christmas?	56
Recovery Time	62
A Memory Flower	67
Off the Shelf	71
Resurrection	76
The Other Side of the Brain	81
Around the Bend	85
House Coats	97
It Runs in the Family	102
Faces of Cork	106
I Live Here	111
Faith of Our Fathers	117
The Last Chapter	121

List of Illustrations

Wild rose
Cow parsley
Gate and field
Song thrush
Dandelion
Common vetch and gorse
Autumn beech leaves
Grasses
Red fox
Bluebells
Thistles
Sweet rocket
Blue tit
Hawthorn berries
Catkins
Meadowsweet and purple loosestrife
Spider
Wood anemones
Primrose
Honeysuckle
Horse chestnut
Dewy webs on gorse
Hawthorn

The Cottage

Nonie's cottage, like herself, was small and welcoming and exuded warmth. She lived a few fields away from my grandmother's farmhouse. During the summer holidays I often stayed with my grandmother, and every Tuesday we took two large baskets of eggs from the free-range hens down to Nonie's cottage, where they were collected by the egg man As we came into the shadowy quietness of her cottage, Nonie would swing the black heavy kettle on the iron crane over the blazing fire in preparation for tea. Then, straightening up, she would come down the little kitchen with outstretched arms and enfold me in a comforting hug. To Nonie, my mother was still a young woman, so this made me think that Nonie was very, very old, but she had none of the austerity of my grandmother and always called us children her *leanaí* ("little ones"). Her snow-white hair was coiled in a knot on top of her head, but little white tendrils escaped and framed her face in a soft halo. Because she and her daughter were its only occupants, and both were fine-boned and dainty as delicate china, the cottage had the aura of a feminine haven. Long white nightdresses edged with lace often blew on the clothes line or hung airing by the fire beside hand-embroidered pillow cases and lace tablecloths. Crocheting and lace-making were Nonie's great loves, and her high-necked white blouses were always edged with lace; around her shoulders she wore a black crochet shawl, and her long black satin skirt swung clear of her tiny, black, soft leather boots. Her little boots were polished to such a high shine that I could see the firelight reflected on her toe-caps. Her daughter, a cheesemaker in a creamery ten miles away, cycled daily to work and back every night. She was the breadwinner, and her wages, together with Nonie's pension, maintained them in a reasonable degree of comfort.

The inside of the cottage, like the outside, was whitewashed, and the yellow thatch came down snugly over the windows like the peak of an old man's cap sheltering small deep-set eyes. In the thatch over the door grew a rosette-forming, evergreen houseleek which flowered in the summer. As well as looking and smelling good, it had an accompanying legend that it prevented bad luck from entering the house and safeguarded against fire. A half-door, while leaving in the fresh air and sunshine, kept out the multi-coloured hens that pecked industriously on the cobbled yard outside. When Nonie wiped the breadcrumbs off the table into her cupped fist, she tossed them over the half-door to the hens outside who squawked in disagreement over the biggest crumbs. The little window in the front only partially lighted the kitchen because the three-foot-thick mud walls funelled the light, leaving some of the kitchen in shadows that were diffused by the flickering firelight and the light from over the half-door.

On the back wall opposite the window was Nonie's dresser, having the ingenuity of design that provided a decorative showpiece for her entire kitchen collection. The large brown and blue dishes stood at the back of the centre shelf, while smaller plates backed the ones above and below; basins and jugs of various colours stood on the shelves, while smaller jugs and cups hung off the hooks on the shelf fronts or rested in nests of saucers between the basins. The two drawers beneath the wide base separating the top and bottom held all the cutlery, while in the open space below stood the black iron pots and kettles for the open fire. As well as the practical need it fulfilled, Nonie's dresser was a pleasure to look at, with its lustre jugs and flower-patterned bowls. One jug in particular was my favourite. It was cream-coloured with a scatter of pale pink roses and a pink rim and handle, and in this Nonie kept the goat's milk. She had only a small green patch of grass at the front of her cottage, so the goat, together with the donkey which provided Nonie's means of transport, grazed the long acre. The donkey cart sheltered in the open shed at the end of the cottage, its orange shafts and wheels contrasting vividly against the black rick of turf beside it.

At the lower end of Nonie's kitchen a door opened into a small bedroom, and apart from this all the living was done in the kitchen. The little house was heated by two turf fires for which the turf was cut and drawn from the nearest bog. As the man in the house had died many years before, any work requiring male muscle was done by the neighbouring men. It was part of the interlaced system that prevailed at the time and helped those within it to support each other.

Nonie's cottage was a social centre for those going to and coming from town. Walking down the hilly roads, strong boots and protective clothing were needed, and as Nonie's cottage was on the side of the main road it was used as a changing depot. Often bicycles were parked against the donkey cart rather than pushed up a steep hill on a dark, wet winter's night. She provided numerous cups of hot, sweet tea coloured with goat's milk and crisp brown bastable bread (baked in a pot on the open fire), and if stronger sustenance was required you got a speckled brown egg standing in a blue china eggcup.

Now the smoke no longer curls from the chimney of Nonie's cottage, for the roof is long gone and the birds build their nests in the ivied gable end that stands as a monument to a noble people who lived in those mud cabins. They were the farm workers who, having no land of their own, helped the farmers till the land. In a primarily agricultural country it was the only means of livelihood available to them. These were the ordinary people of Ireland who, together with the tenant farmers, died of starvation by the roadsides of Ireland during the famine of 1847. Others boarded the coffin ships and sailed for America and Australia, many dying in transit. Of those who made it to a new land, many never returned. Today their descendants come back looking for their family roots amongst the grey stones of Galway and the green hills of Kerry.

Those who survived those terrible times in Ireland became the heart of rural life, their roots buried deep in the soil of the countryside. Some lived on in their thatched mud cabins, while others moved into the cottages built by the British government at the beginning of this century. Accompanying most cottages was an acre of land which they tilled intensively and which provided all that was needed for the kitchen table. If their needs were greater than their acre could supply, they got the use of an adjoining farmer's field. It worked on the basis of a gentlemen's agreement and served both sides well provided that both sides behaved like gentlemen. The design of those cottages varied very little throughout the countryside. They were small, compact, well-built houses, each with a high-pitched slate roof and at the front two windows, one on either side of the front door – though sometimes the two windows were together, to the right or left of the door. The door opened straight into the kitchen, which had an open fire at one end, over which a black iron crane stretched. Off this hung the kettle and cooking pots. Around this fire the family gathered at night as this was often the only source of heat in the cottage.

These people, some of whom still lived in the cabins but the majority in the cottages, were a tough and great-hearted people. They had to be tough to eke out an existence on what was available to them, but their great hearts gave them broad vision. Because their ancestors had suffered much and survived, they knew that they too were survivors. Because of their Celtic origins, a love of music and dance flowed through their veins. Fiddle, concertina and melodeon music, some plaintive and haunting, some bubbling with laughter and gaiety, filled the low-ceilinged cabins and cottages, while the people beat out the rhythm of their hearts in the set-dancing on the stone floors of their mountain homes. The cottages held what they termed "house dances" where the music, singing and dancing were local and spontaneous and the people gathered in from the surrounding countryside. They nurtured and cultivated the old customs of our race, for the cottages of Ireland were the storehouses of our traditional singing and dancing.

Emigration had always been part of Irish life, and when economic depression peaked, as it did in the 1930s and 1950s, so did emigration. Many of the children from our cottages emigrated to England and America and sent home much-needed money. Young boys from the bosoms of large families and close communities went to the wild and lonely plains of Oregon, where they herded sheep in total isolation for many months. What terrible loneliness must have eaten into the marrow of their bones. And when the dollars came back across the Atlantic to help those at home, was it ever realised what a price in human suffering was paid for them? Girls from quiet hills arrived at Paddington station to work to pay the passages of younger sisters and brothers, either to join them or to go further afield to America. When returning Americans come tracing their long-lost ancestors, we might bear in mind that it could be that the dollars of their forefathers kept the heart alive in rural Ireland.

Very few cottages are now in their original state. The economic boom of the 1970s blew out gable ends for extensions and the little cottages mushroomed into much larger homes. Some were abandoned for modern, labour-saving bungalows, and now you will see in rural Ireland the shells of little cottages standing like ghosts in the shadows of new houses. The people who are now seeking out these cottages to restore them are often returning emigrants or people fulfilling a dream of escaping from the stress of living in the fast lane. But the important thing is that our Irish cottages should be alive with the sound of human voices and have smoke curling from the chimneys, not dotting our landscape like quiet grey shadows of another day. Any cottage that sheltered many generations has a past, and there is about an old cottage a sense of timelessness and relaxation that enriches the lives of the occupants. Old stones that have absorbed years of living, sunshine and rain make soothing companions.

> Memory on its
> Soft grey clouds
> Wafting through the rooms,
> Webbing here
> The part of me
> That belongs,
> The living that was blended
> Through these stones;
> So I take with me
> Past soul of this house,
> And leave behind
> Part of mine.

From *Close to the Earth* by Alice Taylor (Brandon, 1988)

The Hatching House

A S YOU PUSHED open the old door it dragged along the floor and you had to lift it up slightly. The house appeared to be in total darkness, but as your eyes grew accustomed to the lack of light you gradually became aware that you were not alone. Slits of wintery sunlight filtered in through the straggling ivy that covered the only window, and in the semi-gloom the outline of an old stone boiler with its rusty door hanging off one hinge stood out from the side wall. At first there appeared to be nothing else in the house, but gradually you saw them, sitting in hatching boxes around by the walls of the old stone house, and your nose absorbed the smell of hens, hay and hatching: a smell full of moist feathers, warm eggs and hay darned with down. Along by the walls the broody hens sat motionless in a hypnotic state, their wings in a maternal spread covering their past products and their future families.

They had left outside the everyday life of the farmyard and were absorbed in their maternal mission in the warm semi-darkness of this womblike house. When you approached them they caoined plaintively, and when you touched them their feathers rose gently in protest and their wings spread out to protect their eggs. So complete was their detachment from normality that they forgot about the need to eat and drink, and they had to be lifted off their eggs for sustenance. They did not want to be disturbed. When you put your hands under their wings to lift them out, they felt warm, heavy and sensuous. Their copulation experience in the farmyard where the cock had distributed his favours had appeared to bring them little pleasure, but now alone in their hatching boxes, their limp languid bodies were relaxed in a post-orgasmic condition. They were enjoying the solitary experience of long tranquil days and nights sitting in their warm, hay-filled boxes, completely sedated by the drowsiness of broody hatching.

Outside in the farmyard the cows heavy with calf moved slowly. The whole farmyard was engrossed in the reproductive cycle. When calving began, a day and night vigil had to be maintained to ensure safe delivery. The cows then regained their agility and the calves, after the first few hours of uncertainty on their feet, danced around their straw-filled house and bellowed impatiently when their stomachs told them that it was time to be fed. They plunged their heads into the buckets of milk and sucked and spluttered, blowing milky bubbles in all directions until they had to come up for air. When the milk was all gone they thumped the buckets with their heads and raced around the house full of the joy of a full belly and a warm bed. If you rubbed your hand down along their soft baby faces, they curled out their long tongues and pulled your fingers into their mouths. At night they lay close together and sometimes one sucked a companion's ear like a baby needing the comfort of a soother.

During the winter the calf house had been a dull silent place, but with the arrival of the baby calves it became the focal point of the farmyard with morning and night feeds and each new arrival needing special treatment until he could look after himself. When they were a few weeks old they graduated into another house. As the days grew longer the number of calves increased until bouncing, bellowing calves filled every available corner.

Once calving was over peace and tranquillity returned to the stalls where the cows stood chewing the cud. In the rafters above their heads, the first swallows swished in to their earth-encrusted nests and started to spring clean after their long winter absence. They wasted no time, and soon the drab grey nests had fresh white feathery bedding peeping out over the tops. All along the rafters their little nests clung to high corners, but each resident seemed to know his own home and flew busily back and forth. The swallows confirmed that the winter was finally gone and that the countryside was about to burst into new life.

In a field down by the river the sheep turned a shady corner into a delivery ward, and when the lambs, after the first few staggering steps, found their food supply, they never rambled far from the woolly comfort of mother. Sometimes, however, the demand exceeded the supply and a lamb had to be brought to the kitchen and bottle fed by the warmth of the fire. He soon returned to the fold where a foster mother was introduced, and after a few days he joined the others and kicked his heels, dancing around in the spring sunshine.

In the wooded fort behind the house the trees were losing their old grey appearance and a soft green veil was beginning to cover their gaunt limbs. Beneath them the bluebells were bursting up through the brown, faded leaves that had fluttered down the previous autumn. They had overwintered on the earth, and she had soaked up their sap and regenerated new life into the many roots that stretched down to her for sustenance. On the surface all appeared to have died in the dark crucifixion of winter, but hidden from our eyes the wonder of nature underneath the soil was turning death into resurrection. The farmers who worked close to the earth were tuned into this miracle of creation and began spring ploughing. During cold bleak days they entrusted seeds to the dark brown earth where they knew that they were in safe keeping.

As the days commemorating the glory of the risen Christ drew near, the seeds too rose out of the earth as a tribute to the glory of God and creation. All over the farm and the countryside, the exuberance of nature celebrated the wonder of creation. Pale green buds poked their tentative heads out through gaunt grey branches and gradually emerged in a profusion of swirling leaves. The birds who had been silenced by the bare branches and the chilly days of winter found new voices and sang songs of praise.

In the hatching house the chickens finally chirped their way out through the crumbling shells and filled the nests with clusters of yellow fluff. They were soft and bright eyed and did not belong in the dark hatching house of winter that smelt of old hay and dehydrated shells. They were part of the new life that was emerging all over the farmyard and belonged to the welcoming world outside that was full of sunshine and singing birds. The hens then turned from broody hatchers into businesslike mothers. They led their broods around the farmyard and protected them from enquiring attention of other occupants with shrill shrieks. They scratched in sheltered corners for tasty morsels, and when we brought chicken mash they supervised meal times and drove away would-be interlopers. When they rested they spread out their wings and the chickens snuggled in beneath them. From the shelter of mother's wings, the chicks poked out their little heads and watched the other fowl and animals in the farmyard around them.

Spring, through the miracle of nature, was busy removing the dark cloak of winter from our world, and when we looked around there awoke in us a sense of appreciation for the transformation. There was a new spurt of vibrancy in the air, and we felt the urge to walk in the fort and to pick the bluebells spread like a blue tablecloth over the mounds and hollows of the old fort.

The chickens were growing long legged and losing their baby look. Strong wing feathers were growing through the soft yellow down, and soon they would be too big to snuggle under mother hen. The first night that they would be able to fly up and join her on the perch in the hen house, she would know that her mothering role was over for another year.

In the old stone house at the end of the yard, the nest boxes were emptied and stacked on top of each other in the corner. The floor was brushed and then washed with swirling buckets of water. It would be another year before it would be again turned into a hatching house.

Green Fields

WHEN I TOLD my sister that I had got a copy of *Green Fields*, she sighed in ecstasy. "Oh, Stephen Rynne," she breathed. "I remember him on radio years ago. His powers of observation and descriptive passages were marvellous. He was the man of the countryside with a wonderful mind and a voice to match."

"How come I cannot remember him?" I asked in a puzzled voice. After all, we had grown up together listening to the same radio.

"You were a slow developer," she informed me. "It took you a long time to wake up to the values of life."

As I read *Green Fields* I had to agree with her. Sisters are seldom wrong.

You open the gate on to Cloonmore, the farm of Stephen Rynne, when you open *Green Fields*. The thresher is coming down the avenue followed by a cortège of tired men, and as it waddles along Stephen Rynne takes you back over the previous few days when these same men stretched every sinew to feed this then roaring monster. Now both men and thresher are sedated with tiredness.

It is the end of the farming season, but it is our introduction to life on the Rynne farm before the advent of the electric fence, the tractor or any of the modern methods of farming. It would be too easy to say that the modern methods destroyed this way of life, but the real difference lies in the man. Stephen

Rynne has the soul of a land lover and is alive to every wildlife ripple on his farm. He is a farmer, but he is also a naturalist and a real countryman at heart. His mind immersed in the beauty which surrounds him, he picks up his paint brush to capture it in watercolour, and with his wonderful mastery of language these pictures become alive on the pages of his book. There are passages to be re-read and savoured like vintage wine, because Rynne paints the seasonal changes of the countryside in dramatic sweeping landscapes, but he also includes little country cameos that will cause you to hold your breath and smile in appreciation. If you are a lover of nature Rynne will delight you, and if to you the countryside is unknown territory, Rynne will reveal to you its hidden face. *Green Fields* should be in every farmhouse in the country, and if children are introduced to him they will look at the countryside with enlightened minds and seeing eyes.

Give yourself time to fall into the soothing tempo of Rynne. He does not grab you by the scruff of the neck, but rather leads you gently through the fields of Cloonmore; gradually you are soothed and slowed down to his pace. "There are no days so pleasant as those on which I stay at home and do ordinary things. I might have gone to Colonel Hawthorn's auction today at Belsize House; I ought certainly to have gone to Mrs Maher's funeral, or, if I were the sort of Irishman believed typical by most Englishmen, I should have spent the day merrily at the Ballynash races. I remained at home and pottered shamelessly."

Cloonmore, once owned by the Devonshires, is no mean farm. Stephen Rynne is not a descendant but has purchased the land, and the battle to make ends meet is a constant struggle, though you are aware that the lifestyle here is well sustained and comfortable as becomes the standards and traditions of such a holding. Rynne is a batchelor, so his housekeeper Mrs Meehan presides over the kitchen and the household chores and keeps a motherly eye on him. You get the impression that their relationship is that of a kindly aunt and slightly irresponsible nephew. His productive kitchen garden and well-cared-for apple trees produce an abundant harvest which Mrs Meehan's good housekeeping converts into saleable products that bring in much needed revenue. One feels that there are touches of Mrs Beaton about this housekeeper who single-handedly keeps the wheels of this farmhouse running smoothly. One can almost smell the simmering pots and the homemade furniture polish and see her ample figure ironing the linen sheets smelling of the world outside.

Out in the farmyard an Englishman called Duggie Sparrow looks after the poultry. When Stephen takes to his bed with the 'flu, or rather when Mrs Meehan gives him no choice but to do so, Duggie is left to sell some bonhams and is totally at a loss in handling the mental dexterity of the shrewd countrywoman who comes to purchase. Duggie with his correct English behaviour contrasts vividly with the easygoing attitude of the other farm workers, Mick, John, Jimmy and Joe, who are totally at one with the land and animals and who allow the requirements of both to dictate their work pace, rather than the owner. Farm plans and decisions are discussed in the farm workshop after dinner and "it is the nearest approach we have to a board meeting". This farmer treats his workers and his animals with consideration and kindness. When the sheep are lost in the snow, gruelling hours are spent trying to dig them out and bring them to safety, and when one is discovered days afterwards, the efforts spent on its rescue far outweigh the commercial value of the sheep.

But we are also taken outside Cloonmore: to the cattle fair with a neighbour, Pat Mangan, and to the Dublin market, for example. The most colourful outing, however, is to the bog where there is a turf-cutting contest going on and one of the guests is President de Valera. Rynne has an eye for every detail, even the hats: "Here are hats that have seen prosperity and adversity, gone from black or brown to green and pinkish hues, lapsed from hat box shapes to an utter unshapliness. But there are fine faces under them; shrewd, keen, honest, hardworking, and innocent faces."

21

At night Stephen Rynne takes refuge in his books and states, "But for Cobbett's *Rural Rides and Advice to Young Men*, Darwin's *Voyage of the Beagle*, and Joseph Joubert's *Thoughts*, the long winter nights would be too long by streets." He expresses a deep regret that we cannot claim Cobbett as one of our own. It is at night also that he studies the catalogues to order his young trees to create shelter belts around the farm. Trees are his great love and he goes into minute detail about the young and the old ones around Cloonmore.

He does not romanticise the hardships of farming, but his appreciation of nature and his wonderfully observant eye make this a delightful book. It could only have been written by a man who loved the countryside and never lost his sense of wonder at the unfolding drama of nature. This is an ideal book for beneath your pillow, because after a few chapters of Rynne you will feel that all is well and you will sleep like one of the birds that fly so joyfully through this book.

But we will leave the last word to the man himself.

"When I am dead, send a wreath of furze. Plant it over me; let it rip wantonly on my grave; let the artillery of its seed popping be my last post, and its scent my incense."

Rural Reading

INTO OUR HOUSE every day came the *Cork Examiner*.
My father could not survive a day without "the paper"
and he read it in great detail. He always read the death
column (I wondered at the time how anyone could find that
interesting) and then my mother and himself discussed the
death of anyone they knew and the possibility that they
might be related to us through some far flung family branch.
If so, my mother could then decide that the funeral merited
the attendance of a family member, a decision with which my
father was not always in agreement. He would declare that a
funeral was a row of mad men following a dead man, while
my mother considered attending a funeral to be one of the
corporal works of mercy. There was no solution to that argu-
ment. In the end we were often dispatched across the fields
to the old graveyard to attend the funeral of an unknown
body, and my father must have sometimes regretted his
reading of the death column.

Once a week we got the *Cork Weekly Examiner* which published readers' letters and poems that we read with great
interest. The Sunday papers and the *Irish Catholic* came at the
weekends, and also the *Radio Review*. The *Irish Catholic* was sold
by a thin, pale-faced man who stood in a large timber box,
like a miniature horse box, which was parked outside the
chapel. It had a hinged door that fell forward and formed his
counter. My mother and this delicate looking man, whom I

considered to be very old, had long discussions as to the state of his mother's health. It surprised me that his mother could still be alive, because when you are about ten years old you consider anyone over forty to be on the verge of senile decay. I always hoped that one Sunday morning his mother would be there, propped up inside in the box. But she was to remain a shrouded mystery though I felt that I knew her quite well. Every Sunday I listened with curiosity to her weekly health bulletin. To me the state of her health was far more interesting than anything that the Catholic paper had to offer.

The Sunday papers were sold by a large jolly lady who wore a plunging neckline beneath rows of chins that wobbled when she threw back her head to laugh heartily. Her elocution was perfect and her eyes behind her gold rimmed spectacles sparkled with merriment as she traded good humoured exchanges with her customers. She presided behind a wide counter that was draped with a bewildering selection of papers, but my mother was not confused by variety of choice. There was no possibility that she would purchase an English newspaper and corrupt her family with foreign notions! But she felt that our innocent minds were safe perusing the pages of the *Sunday Press*. As I stood outside the counter I ran my eye over the dramatic headlines about murder and sex in what I considered the more exciting papers. I thought that my mother's taste in newspapers was very tame.

Her next port of call was the local pub, not to slake her thirst but to purchase *The Messenger*. The lady behind the pub counter was skeleton thin and wore a hand-knitted cardigan with sleeves that never quite made it to her bony wrists. Her foxy hair streaked with grey was pulled back tightly into a hard knot at the base of her skull, which gave her face a stretched look. She looked at life over her spectacles. When she saw my mother arrive in the door she disappeared into a little sectioned-off portion of the counter. She emerged bearing in front of her in both hands the red-covered *Messenger*. I never heard the conversation that took place between herself and my mother because it was exchanged in whispers, which made me think that the scandals of the town were buried in her bosom.

My brother, however, was a dedicated devotee of the *Reader's Digest* which he received monthly by post, and he signed us on for the *Junior Digest*. Every week he bought *Ireland's Own* from which we learned songs, tested our brain power with riddles and the flexibility of our tongues with tongue twisters and absorbed with exquisite horror the exploits of Kitty the Hare.

From school every month we brought *The Far East*, and when we were half-ways home in the summer, we sat on top of Dave's Hill and read Pudsy. That Pudsy had a problem with his spelling made him a fellow sufferer in our quest for education.

Maybe the fact that *The Far East*, *The Messenger*, the *Cork Examiner*, the *Reader's Digest* and *Ireland's Own* are still on sale proves that they have stood the test of time.

A Woman with a Mission

TODAY CRAFT SHOPS and potteries are to be found in remote parts of rural Ireland, and it is wonderful that so many of our crafts have been preserved. One of the people who helped to bring this about was Muriel Gahan, a woman of great foresight. Her philosophy of life was "Deeds not Words", and when a book was finally written about her this became its title.

She was born in October 1897 in a house called Magherabeg on the outskirts of Donegal town. Her grandfather, Frederick Gahan, was county engineer for Donegal. His mother had been a Townsend from Cork and he married a Jane Townsend. Their son, Frederick George Townsend Gahan, Muriel's father, followed in his father's footsteps and became a civil engineer, while three of his four brothers became Church of Ireland clergymen. Muriel's father worked first with the Cavan and Leitrim Light Railway Company, but when the Congested Districts Board (CDB) was established in 1891, in an effort by the government to improve living conditions in the poorest areas of the west of Ireland, he was offered a job with it. In 1900 the family moved to Castlebar, Co. Mayo.

The great influence on her of her father's work and the ten years Muriel Gahan spent as a small child in Castlebar played a crucial part in her later development. Mayo's extraordinary beauty was imprinted on Muriel Gahan's psyche at an early age, but the poverty that she witnessed marked her deeply.

Muriel's travels first began with her father when he set off to visit projects in the far reaches of Mayo. As they travelled along, Gahan would have talked to his children about the CDB's attempt to develop the crafts at the turn of the century. It was no easier at this time than when Muriel tried to revive them forty years on, but her father had passed on the fostering torch to his young daughter at an early age.

She had ten magic years in the freedom of Mayo but that came to an end in 1910 when, at the age of thirteen, she was sent to St Winfred's school for girls near Bangor in North Wales. Three years later when her mother and the children moved to Dublin, she was sent to Alexandra College. Muriel always recognised that it was "the Alexandra" that provided any education that she got. "They taught us to be leaders," she would say, adding with a mischievous smile, "leaders of what, I'm not quite sure." Although radical and progressive in educational matters, the college's politics were conservative and Unionist. Here she made many friends including Livic Crookshank who even at this early stage was sensitive to social issues and interested in co-operation as a way of encouraging people to help themselves toward a better life.

Muriel started work as a painter with a decorating firm, and it was her skills as an interior decorator that led her to Miss Lucy Franks, to the society of United Irishwomen (UI) and to the Royal Dublin Society, and those meetings in turn determined a lifelong dedication to the people of rural Ireland. The RDS had a long tradition of supporting rural industry and traditional crafts going back to its foundation in 1731. The 1929 Spring Show was an eye opener for Muriel. There she got to know people like Maine Jellet, the modernist artist, and Vida Lentaigne, an active United Irishwoman who lived in the house at Termonfeckin which twenty-five years on would become An Grianán. Muriel became a member of the UI and at the request of Lucy Franks searched Mayo to find a weaver willing to demonstrate the weaving of homespun tweed for the 1930 Spring Show. This search for a weaver and her eventual discovery of Patrick Madden in Ballycroy, Co . Mayo, led directly to the idea of setting up a craft depot in Dublin to provide an outlet for isolated craftworkers. That in turn developed into the creation of The Country Shop, for years the nerve centre of so much that was being achieved in the country, both for the crafts and for the women.

I regret that I never had the pleasure of visiting The Country Shop in St Stephen's Green or meeting this wonderful woman who did so much for the crafts of Ireland and who was instrumental in the setting up of Country Markets, the ICA and An Grianán.

She died in 1995, and her time spanned almost a century of Irish life which saw great changes during which she worked tirelessly to preserve the old rural crafts. She was a well-to-do Protestant lady who could have engaged herself in many ways but who chose to promote the culture of her less-well-off fellow countrywomen who were mostly of a different persuasion. She was also surrounded by a group of determined women. Geraldine Mitchell, who wrote the life of Muriel Gahan, *Deeds not Words*, painted a very vivid picture of them and their time.

The Women of Shawls

ER DARK EYES glinted from the mysterious depths of a tartan shawl that draped down over a square basket overflowing with brown scapulars, holy pictures and balls of camphor.

"Is the woman of the house inside?" she asked, whipping her shawl tighter around her.

I was twelve years of age and she was as old as time. We knew them as the tinkers, a name derived from their craft of tinsmiths. They called themselves the travelling people, a more fitting, poetic and descriptive title.

The travelling women of my childhood are today wearing jeans, sneakers and driving Hiace vans. Their knocks on farmhouse doors are usually answered by old people. If there is a young woman of the house, she probably has a job in the nearest big town because a second income is needed to set beside the "set aside". So while our Celtic Tiger is busy swishing his tail around our overcrowded cities and large towns, the sheep dogs of rural Ireland are wailing in desolate farmyards.

Outside influences over which we had little control changed things, but we also put our shoulder under the coffin. We closed our small rural schools, the lifeblood of our community, and bussed our children into the big towns. We decided that big was best and forgot that small is beautiful and often more efficient. It was not without irony that simultaneously throughout rural Ireland, barnlike, carpet-covered funeral parlours sprouted up. Our schools moved out and our funeral parlours moved in. We were no longer comfortable with our dead, and instead of burying them decently we covered them with green plastic sheets.

The small rural school was the heartbeat of a community. When the doors opened in the evening the sound of young voices filled the air with vibrancy and laughter. With the school closures, the young people take the bus in the dark of the morning and come home in the dusk of the evening. Our living landscape that should encompass its own education is no longer seen as a fitting background. The way forward to a better Ireland is outside their local community. Their circle of friends has become larger and less intimate, the pool too big to fish out the bullies. Illiteracy can more easily slip through a wide net. It was the thin end of the wedge that cracked open the skull of rural Ireland. The school was the pivot around which parents could revolve and communicate.

One of the saddest problems in rural Ireland today is loneliness. As a people we engaged in casual rather than formal socialising. TV eroded the casual calling that was part of our way of doing things and we never took formal entertaining on board. So we are left with a large void, which can sometimes be tinged with fear. It was deemed economically prudent to close down rural barracks, removing the local guard who had his finger on the pulse of his people. He was a crime prevention officer before we ever heard of that slick term. We had it, but we wiped it out with the swipe of a bureaucratic pen. The same pen was applied with the equal vigour to our rural post offices, but then the worm finally turned and we called halt. John Healy would have been proud of us.

About two years ago a woman came to see me. She was a total stranger.

"Why don't you write about emigration?" she demanded.

"I never emigrated," I told her, "and it is difficult to write about something outside your own experience.

"Well, this is my experience," she told me, "so will you please tell people my story. I have two sons who were very good students. One wanted to stay at home and become a farmer and the other wanted to go to university, and that was fine by my husband and me. We have a good sized farm and live comfortable off it. The boys' headmaster told us at a parents' meeting that our two boys would get very high point ratings and were guaranteed a place in university. We explained that one lad wanted to go farming, and the teacher made us feel that farming was a waste of brain power. But we came home and discussed it again and came to the same conclusion. So one lad went to university and the other stayed farming. Today I am on my way home from the airport after waving the university graduate off to New York, and if I had listened to that teacher I would be waving the two of them off and selling my farm. What is wrong with us in Ireland that we have so demeaned farming as a way of life?"

She was an angry, puzzled woman. I have sometimes thought of those two sons and wondered that if the two of them had emigrated would the one who had the farming heart come back one day in his declining years and stand at the gate of his farm, then owned by someone else, and feel that he had lost his birthright? Our roots do not always react with reason.

Last year the radio and newspapers overflowed with angry reaction to the depiction of Ireland on "Eastenders". We were not amused! But we Irish do it to ourselves. Recently, the Ploughing Championship was highlighted with a photograph of a one-toothed man. The only reason he was there was the glory of his one tooth. If it had appeared in an English publication we would have been frothing at the mouth with annoyance.

Kavanagh probed the soul of the country when he wrote

> We are a dark people,
> Our eyes are ever turned
> Inwards

34

Watching the liar who twists
The hill-paths awry.

Tarry Flynn and *The Green Fool* make us very aware of who we are. Kavanagh had the love–hate relationship with the land that is part of the Irish psyche, but he could stir up the poetry that is buried in the muddied waters of our subconscious. Had we studied Kavanagh we would never have levelled our ditches and hedgerows to make pasture to feed extra cows and pour milk into overflowing milk lakes.

If the travelling woman with the tartan shawl now came looking for the woman of the house in rural Ireland, she would get no reply at many doors. I have never forgotten her and the magic of her large wicker basket. It was a time when money was scarce and hard work was the order of the day, and the only wealth was the land and its people. They worked together, trusted and betrayed each other and sometimes got embroiled in bitter conflicts over land boundaries and water rights. Struggles within families overflowed into the local community and even dark secrets seeped out. The women with the shawls saw it all as they carried their baskets of covered treasure from door to door.

Christmas in the Village Shop

U NCLE JACKY KEPT an old battered tin bucket under the table in the back kitchen. Into it went all the leftovers after the meals: bits of bread, potato skins and egg shells. When Aunty Peg was clearing away after the tea, she emptied the *dríodar* from the bottom of the cups into the bucket where it soaked into the waste bread and softened it. This waste disposal unit was known as the hen's bucket

The hens lived in a "Jacky-made" galvanised-iron house under the trees at the top of the garden. Morning and evening he climbed the steep garden path that wound between his flowers, vegetables and old apple trees to bring sustenance to his free range hens who had the run of the grove, but they sometimes overran their boundaries and scuffled between his rhubarb rows and scratched out his baby seedlings. He was very tolerant of their misdemeanours and treated them with loving kindness, even if they committed the greatest offence of all, which was to stop laying before Aunty Peg started her Christmas baking. This came about if there was a hard frost in November, but to Aunty Peg that was a lame excuse. When it happened she threatened to wring their necks and reduce them to broth. To Aunty Peg the hens were a necessary evil, and she regularly declared that they were more trouble than they were worth, even though she herself got very little trouble from them. But they justified their existence by providing a regular supply of eggs for her baking, which was her favourite pastime, and this activity peaked at Christmas.

Aunty Peg would never tell you that she had her Christmas baking done. Instead she would say, "I threw the cakes together last night," and that was literally what she did. She never weighed anything, but judged it by "the ball of the eye". Sometimes she forgot them in the oven and they came out a bit charred, but they always tasted divine and far more flavoursome than mine that were weighed and measured to the exact ounce and timed to the last minute in the oven. Before Aunty Peg's cakes had time to mature, they were sampled by old customers invited in to toast the Christmas spirit, and often a second baking session was necessary

When Uncle Jacky's customers came into his little shop to buy their Christmas cards, he helped them to make their choices. Sometimes an address could be forgotten and Jacky would have a record of it in a small red notebook. As the little shop was also the post office, he regarded this as part of the services to be provided. He also wrapped up their parcels for posting.

He did not go in for glittering Christmas decorations. In one shop window he stood a big fat cardboard Santa who, because he had one wobbly leg, had to be propped up at the back with a big bottle of lemonade, but this time-battered Santa smiled kindly at the passers-by. In the other window was a little timber crib with a thatched roof. They probably never saw a thatched stable in Bethlehem, but in our village the crib blended into the Irish environment. Across the low ceiling of the shop, he draped two coloured paper chains that had seen better days.

On Christmas Eve when the village people called to him for bunches of fresh thyme, he ran up the garden for it, sometimes bringing them holly as well and, to the chosen few, some of his Christmas roses.

On Christmas night Aunty Peg lit the big white Christmas candle in the centre of the sitting room table and their Christmas cards were draped on strings above the fireplace and across the old mirrored sideboard. Later they would sit by the fire and she would read out the greetings on the cards to Jacky. But before settling down for the night by the fire, he would go up the garden, whistling happily, to check on his hens and close up their house for the night. Outside the hen house he would stand and look down over his garden and watch the smoke rise from the village chimneys. I often watched him standing up there and knew that for him, our village on that night was Bethlehem. He had Christmas in his heart.

The Forge

THOUGH IT WAS the last day of winter the weather was mild, but late in the afternoon a cold breeze seemed to whip around the village of Innishannon when the news became known that Billy had died quietly in his forge

Billy O'Connell and his forge were so much part of our community that we almost thought both were indestructible. Over the years we had remarked to each other in the village that when he would go a whole way of life would go with him. But it was something for the future, to be taken into account when it would come about; somewhere down the road on a far horizon. Now all of a sudden it was a reality, and it was as if a cornerstone had fallen off the village.

Five generations of Billy's family had worked in that small stone building under the spreading beech tree at the entrance to Dromkeen wood at the western end of the village. Billy began work there as a young lad of fourteen when he and his two brothers were trained by their father Denis, known affectionately as "Poundy". The four of them were kept going shoeing farm horses. It cost five shillings then to shoe a horse, and eight sets was a good day. They worked on an anvil that was over one hundred and fifty years old and, together with the hob, had come from the old Bandon Railway yard. His father had bought them when the yard was scrapped in the early thirties.

In recent times Billy alone remained. His kindly touch over the years had turned the forge into much more than a place for shoeing horses. It had become a focal point in the social life of the parish. Farmers came there on wet days, sometimes to shoe horses but often just to pass the time when it was too wet to work out in the fields. Late at night as Billy continued to work making shoes in preparation for the following day, they came again, soft-voiced, easygoing countrymen. It was heart warming to see them through the forge door, their orange shadows illuminated in the glow of the fire. They sat on pieces of iron or leaned against the stone walls as they discussed horses and racing, the crops, the weather and the state of things in the farming world generally. Billy was not one for long-winded dialogue himself and was content to throw in a passing comment here and there as the conversation flowed around him. He worked almost by instinct and precise measurements were in his fingers and hands. Burning hot iron became exact shapes with a few casual belts of the hammer. When he went to assess an outside job he never carried a measuring tape. He ran an experienced eye over the project and his fingers did the measuring.

He had friends who called regularly, some twice daily, so that it was unusual to find Billy alone in the forge. Children waited there for the bus, and if they missed it Billy would get them a lift from a reliable motorist. Small children came to him with little wheelbarrows and broken bikes, and he welded them back together again. People from the countryside around the forge seldom passed that way without calling in to see Billy to have a chat.

In his father's time and in Billy's earlier days it had been hairy-hoofed farm horses that had clomped in there to have their heavy shoes replaced, but with the departure of the horse from the land that scene changed. Now horse-boxes parked outside and slender-legged, elegant thoroughbreds from a wide circle of riding stables danced in high spirits on the forge floor.

But though the type of horse changed everything else remained the same, even Billy. He never seemed to grow older and always had the same happy, bantering approach to life. He loved his work and it gave him complete fulfilment, and monetary gain was away down on his list of priorities. When the gate of the old graveyard had to be widened, Billy did it free of charge, and it was only one of the many jobs he did just for the satisfaction of seeing a job well done. All around the countryside are samples of Billy's craftsmanship. Because he loved to create he made each horse's shoes individually even when mass production became fashionable. He charged very little for his skills, but then Billy's priorities were not for building kingdoms in this world.

It is sometimes said that a man has to die to be appreciated, but this was not the case with Billy. In the first edition of *Innishannon Candlelight* in 1984 there was an article, "The Place We Call the Forge" by Mary Nolan O'Brien, and in it she wrote:

> One's own place must surely mean different things to different people but when I reflect on Innishannon the place that immediately springs to mind is that unobtrusive building at the entrance to the village; the place we call The Forge or more often referred to as "Billy's". Well to me and many generations before me the forge is firstly an irreplaceable landmark at the entrance to the village. It stands like a lodge at the entrance to a great estate. It has witnessed many changes in the village and surrounding areas over its long life but thankfully has escaped the modern image itself.
>
> When I cast my mind back to the first day I walked to Innishannon school the thing that I can still picture most vividly is that cloud of blue smoke curling from the roof of the forge and fading into the wooded background. Today when I take the same route nothing seems to have changed. The forge with its distinctive sound and smell, its friendly inhabitants and cloud of smoke remains the same. We have good reason to feel indebted to the O'Connell family for keeping this important part of our heritage alive. Long may it remain to keep a watchful eye

on the happenings in the village as it stands at the gateway to our own place.

Now the custodian of our village gateway has been called to higher places and his little lodge stands empty. At his funeral people from all walks of life gathered: the horsemen, the greyhound men, the fishermen and the GAA men. All came to say:

"Billy O'Connell . . . Farewell"

Something to Crow About

MY FAVOURITE WOOD has stone steps leading down into it. I love to go down there, to peel off my ordinary life and walk free, just to stand and absorb the wood life. It is going down into the quiet womb of the earth.

> Let me creep down
> A brown burrow,
> Down into the
> Quiet womb of the earth.
> Deep down where there
> Is only silence.
> Down, down,
> Where velvet darkness
> Clothes the ragged mind
> In a shawl of gentle silence.

Just to stand and absorb the wood life. Down there between the trees is quietness. Nature has a wonderful sense of drama: the trees part at this point of entrance to frame the view. You see through the leafy opening the river curving into the distance below. It is as if the wood is saying, "Look and absorb and let me create your mood so that we can enjoy our shared time together." Watching a river has a calming effect. This river edged with woods is a sheltered silent reflection of the beauty above it.

A mossy bank offers a comfortable seat to sit and watch the swans on the river drift effortlessly along above their wavering reflections. All is well in their world. Feathery heather and drooping moist ferns kiss my ankles. I have always had a special love of ferns with their long, arching, delicate fronds. As children we played beneath them in a field behind our house where they grew to huge heights and created long green tunnels of light

At the bottom of the incline the path runs along the river-bank, and here you can sit and look across at a little quayside village. The village and the small boats tied up along the quay are mirrored in the deep water. I sit and listen to the tidal water lap against the bank as it changes direction.

The day is drawing to a close and the sky is golden through the leafy branches of a great tree. This drooping tree is growing out over the river, its enormous trunk bedded in the riverbank. Its roots must extend as far back into the wood as its branches extend out over the water.

At this time of evening the wood creatures are settling down for the night. I do not see them but they are to be heard scurrying about in the undergrowth. A bird, having planned an early night, flaps in protest at my presence. But of all the birds in the wood at this time of day, the crows are the most interesting. I am not a lover of crows, but in the evening I never tire of watching them as they all head homewards after spending the day in different places. They arrive in little groups like people coming together for a party or a meeting. Theirs is a huge gathering. They come up the river and over the wood, all heading for the same patch of trees. They land in hundreds in a flurry of wings and squawking beaks. There is something almost human about crows at this time of evening. They are gossiping old ladies in black shawls exchanging the day's news.

My grandmother, standing at her front door when she was very old, would watch the crows flying home and say, "The crows are going home to Ahane," which was her girlhood home. As a child I always felt that she wished she could fly home with them and I felt sad for her.

The sound of the evening crows in the wood has to be heard

47

to be believed. The first time that I witnessed this home-coming I thought that it was impossible for crows to make such a racket. While I was trying to convince myself that it had to be more than the crows a gunshot rang out in the distance. Suddenly the wood was silent for one breath-holding moment. You could sense every black head cocked in alarm. Then almost as one, they dismissed the scare and broke forth again louder and more aggressive.

I seldom see a fox in the wood, but one evening last week we came face to face. We were on the same path going in opposite directions when he shot into view. His strong legs were covered in mud as if he had come through a swamp. We took each other totally by surprise when we came eyeball to eyeball. He held me hypnotised in his black and amber eyes. Then, deciding that I had right of way, he stepped aside and melted into the undergrowth. He was gone almost before I realised that he was there.

When I am out of step with myself or my fellow human beings, I need to take time off and go into the woods. I may go in tired and with ragged nerves, but I will come out at the other end soothed and calm.

Herself Upstairs

S HE CAME FOR a month and stayed for thirteen years. She always told me that guests were like fish and smelled after three days, but she herself was a contradiction of that maxim. If I had gone out and searched for somebody to share a small corner of our home for that many years, I do not think that I could have found anybody who would have fitted in as well as she did. But I did not find her; she found me instead.

After her husband had died suddenly, she did not wish to live alone in their house down by the river. She enquired if she could move into a small self-catering apartment in our house for a time until she had her affairs sorted out. I assumed that it would only be for a very short period as she had been used to gracious living. Having grown up in one of the stately homes of Ireland, she had lived afterwards in many different parts of Europe.

When she had been with us for a few weeks, she enquired one day if it would be all right if she got in the phone. Then I realised that she had come to stay. Because she had a double barrel name which was difficult to pronounce, our children christened her Mrs C., and so she became known in our house as Mrs C. or "herself upstairs".

She had a large circle of friends and each day she either went out for lunch or had friends in for dinner or vice versa. She loved good conversation, good wine and good books and was a wonderful talker. She told me that everybody had a duty when in company "to bring their penny to the pool".

She disliked boring people and she herself was the least boring person you could meet. I read somewhere once that Oscar Wilde said that the one offence in life was to be boring. At the time of reading I had thought that it was a very arrogant statement. As I grew older and a little wiser, I realised that it contained great wisdom, because the only people who are really boring are those who have no interest in anything other than themselves. Their world starts with their toes and finishes at their heels and they have no interest beyond that perimeter. All conversations invariably lead back to themselves.

Mrs C. avoided these people like the plague, but if she had them thrust upon her she had her own way of dealing with them. After a visit from a long lost school friend who brought a handbag full of photographs of her grandchildren, she informed me that she had never spent a more boring afternoon, poring over toothless babies and gowned graduates who all looked the same after viewing the first two. When the same lady returned the following day with another cargo of photographs, she was told in no uncertain fashion to "Put them away. There is nothing as boring as other people's grandchildren."

She always maintained that it was a bad thing to be too tolerant because if you put up with too much in life you then had too much put upon you. She had decided that one of the privileges of old age was that you did not have to tolerate many of the things that you felt you had to when you were younger.

"I may not have that much time left, so I must make good use of it," she told me.

And she did just that despite the fact that her clock of life had gone well over eighty.

One morning a friend of mine who was doing early morning shopping in our supermarket met Mrs C. dressed up to the nines, and my friend, thinking that she was going into Cork shopping, asked, "Are you going out for the day?

"Yes, my dear," she was told. "I am going to Russia."

She had decided to go to Russia to see the art galleries before she got older and the journey might be a bit too much for her – this at an age when most people would have decided that long distance travel was no longer feasible. But she was not like most people, and even when the frailties of old age finally caught up with her and she had to have major surgery on one of her legs, she still handled it with style. She booked a private room in a top class hospital where her many friends surrounded her with flowers. She reclined in state in the midst of them in a stunning pink silk dressing gown bought specially for the occasion. Fate however dealt her a rough blow. After she came home, it was discovered that another operation was necessary on the other leg. I worried at that point that this was a tough fence to clear and that she might not make it, but she cleared it with flying colours. A month afterwards she was on a plane to London to do her Christmas shopping in Harrods. Whereas with many people ill health becomes the central theme of their old age, with Mrs C. it was something to be got over and put behind her so that she could get back to quality living as fast as possible.

Letter writing was something which she enjoyed and she kept in touch with friends all over the world. Every morning I brought her post upstairs, together with the London *Times* which was her daily paper. She breakfasted in bed, reading her letters and, through the window at the end of her bed, enjoying watching our two dogs playing in the garden and the deliveries coming through the yard to the back door of the shop. Through her sitting room window at the front she watched people come and go to the pub across the road. The fact that some men who brought their wives or girl friends to the pub never even waited for them to get out of the car but trotted off into the pub ahead of them never ceased to amaze her.

One day as I sat chatting with her an elderly local couple who had moved in to live together rather late in life came out the pub door.

"Difficult to figure out the reason for that union," she commented drily, "but I doubt that she acquired him for his sexual prowess."

She enjoyed young people, and because she was interested in everything that went on around her she had many young friends, including my children, especially one of them with whom she had long and complicated arguments about religion and politics. When I once asked her about these long debating sessions, she told me, "I enjoy the stimulation of the young. The old should always surround themselves with the young. Too many old people together depress each other."

She watched every race meeting, and rugby, tennis and golf match on television, and even GAA matches about which she knew very little. Politicians, however, annoyed her intensely, and one evening as the television news reported some political scandal, she informed me with vehemence, "That Dáil is full of fraudulent illiterates!"

Small boned and pencil slim, a great beauty in her day, in old age she still dressed elegantly. Whenever I bought new clothes she was my first port of call for comment. I valued her opinion because she had a great eye for detail and was very honest and direct in her approval or disapproval. She disapproved highly of my tendency to wear long floral skirts.

"You have a good figure and nice legs. Why do you bury them under those long mopey skirts?" she would ask me.

She was always a picture of Parisian elegance herself and even when confined to bed succeeded in looking well.

A great believer in self-discipline, she was the perfect time keeper, and unpunctual people annoyed her intensely. However, she did not want them to err on the other side either. Once when she was teaching two of my children how to play bridge, she invited them to come at a certain time, and when they presented themselves five minutes too early, they were sent away and told to come back at the correct time. Part of her self-discipline was to get up every morning at a certain time. One cold winter's morning when I suggested her staying in bed a little longer as it was such a miserable morning, she told me, "When you are my age that is the last thing to do because that is the thin edge of the wedge, and it's downhill from there on. If you, my dear, take a lie in on a morning, you just have to get out of it the morning after, but I do not have to, so I have to discipline myself."

My mother was a late night person and got a second wind after midnight. Two of my children have inherited the trait, and generally we tend to go to bed late at night. Mrs C.'s comment on this was, "The Irish are too lazy to go to bed."

Late at night when I sit by the fire chatting or stuck in a good book or simply gazing into the fire, I know exactly what she meant.

Because she had such an active social life and was out so often in her car, I sometimes wondered if the day came when this was no longer possible how she would handle it. I thought that she would find being confined to barracks very frustrating. But again she surprised me and coped amazingly well. Because she never complained even when she was not feeling too good but was always far more interested in the world outside her world and never mentioned her pains and aches, I asked her one day, "How come you never complain?"

She leant back against her pillows and pinned her piercing blues eyes on me and said slowly, "My mother once told me, 'Never indulge in self-pity,' she said; 'it destroys yourself and alienates people.'

It was good advice and she followed it to the letter. She was an example of how to grow old gracefully, and when the end drew near she instructed, "The nearest patch with the least possible amount of fuss."

What Have We Done to Christmas?

I N MID-NOVEMBER I read the following extract from an article by Maureen Fox in the *Cork Examiner*:

> Do you know something? I am perfectly convinced that the one official holiday in the entire year that is most dreaded is Christmas! Year after year I hear about family quarrels, violence, drunkenness, stress and afterwards facing the huge debts that have been run up in what should be a holy and Christian celebration.
>
> And yet another indicator of what Christmas has become is that it is one of the busiest times of the year for the Samaritans.

That article gave food for thought. Maybe that is what good journalism is all about. It made me think of my mother sprinkling us with holy water as my father lit the Christmas candle. Looking back I realise now that my mother made Christmas out of very little, but she infused it with a sense of anticipation and a depth of spirituality. She involved her children in the preparation of the house and never took her eye off the real reason for all the fuss. What have we done to Christmas? Have we taken the child out of Christmas and left a vacuum in the crib?

Why do we sometimes think that because our parents did something in a certain way that it must be old fashioned and backward? Is it because they had no experts to advise them on the correct procedures? But some of their ways of doing things were tried and tested by previous generations and had built into them the wisdom of human experience. They did not always get it right, but often they had their priorities in good order.

Most people went to confession for Christmas. They unburdened themselves of their problems to someone who was committed to silence. They looked after the inner man first. If I am not at peace and at one with myself no amount of gift wrapping or alcohol can ease the pain of inner turmoil. This feast is all about Jesus in the crib and if we take him out of it and try to fill it with shopping, rushing and yelling "Happy Christmas" at each other, we are only codding ourselves. The sad thing is, we can never succeed in fully fooling ourselves, and there is always a gap where the pain slips in. Often when there is pain within we try to sedate ourselves in many ways, but we never quite succeed.

As the whirl that is today's Christmas draws in around us and we ride the crest of the wave of commercialism, it is difficult to remember the deeper and real meaning of Christmas. It is a time of baking, cleaning and shopping, and we all enjoy the buzz that it brings to the dark winter days. A long winter without the warmth of Christmas in the middle of it would be a dismal prospect. The preparations and the celebrations are great, but they are more satisfying when we raise our eyes higher than our stomachs and reach into the rich spirituality of the holy time.

As a child the highlight of my Christmas was the lighting of the Christmas candle. It stood tall and white on the kitchen window and lit up windows of wonder down the corridors of my child's mind. We have come a long way from the candle in the turnip! Maybe we need to go a little way back down that road and bring home some of the old rituals and magic into Christmas. We all have the glittering Christmas tree and it brightens up every home; how lovely it would be if we had the crib as well. Even a very simple crib brings the heart of Christmas into the home.

Setting up the crib is my favourite part of getting the

house ready for Christmas. The first step is a visit to Shippool wood the Sunday before Christmas to gather holly, ivy, moss, ferns and interesting looking battered bits of fallen branches; in fact anything that might come my way. It is a voyage of discovery because every year the findings are different. If you live near a wood you can have a real live crib. Sometimes it may become more alive than you planned, as it is difficult to transport moist moss without some enclosed passengers. However that only adds to the authenticity, as I am sure that the stable at Bethlehem was not squeaky clean either. The basis of my crib is a large piece of driftwood that I rescued from the mouth of the Feale many years ago. It has long arching white arms stretching from a cavelike base, and when it is covered with moss and ferns I have the side of a Bethlehem hill. From then on it's a labour of love as out come battered shepherds and a comfortable looking cow who would not conform to modern farming methods. My crib figures have been with me for many years and like myself they are showing signs of the passage of time. Children have played with them down through the years, so St Joseph's beard is less than perfect and one wise man has lost his head. When I inherited another crib set from a very dear friend, those figures too move in, so my crib takes a bit of explaining. Over the years I have collected many wooden animals and birds which are all encompassed in the layout. When it is finished it looks a bit like animal farm, but who is to say but that all the animals came that night to celebrate.

Christmas is a time for candles to symbolise the coming of divine light into our lives. The lighting of the Christmas candle is the unveiling of the holy season. It is a Kerry custom to put a lighted candle in every window of the house, and I have adopted this custom because I love candlelight and rejoice in the wonderful variety of candles now available. As we keep bees and have wax available, if we get our act together in time we make our own pure wax Christmas candles. Pure wax candles have a wonderful texture and light with a steady clean yellow flame.

When Scrooge opened his purse he discovered the real meaning of Christmas, that there is joy in giving and receiving. There is no gift that touches the heart of the receiver more than a gift into which a lot of thought is put and, of course, the ultimate here is something that you have made or grown yourself. It is wonderful to get a fine brown cake from a good baker or a pot of homemade jam. One of the best Christmas gifts I ever got was a box of homemade mince pies when the whole house was in disarray with illness. I will never forget the thoughtfulness of the generous giver who gave up her valuable time to make the mince pies. Every Christmas a friend gives me a pot of homemade blackberry jam. Blackberry jam tastes lovely at Christmas! Maybe the time put into these gifts is what makes them so special. And if somebody gives an unexpected present as a token of appreciation, it is a pity to spoil the spontaneity of their impulse by giving one in return. There is generosity in accepting as well as giving. Some people are generous givers but very poor receivers. Gifts given and received with love are what Christmas is all about, and nothing kills its spirit more effectively than duty presents.

The best part of Christmas night is the time we spend on our own with the time to go out for even a short walk, to look up at the stars and know that those same stars shone down on Bethlehem on that first Christmas night. Because the first Christmas took place out in the quietness of the country under the night sky, I need to give myself time to wind down and feel the essence of Christmas that is out in the stillness of the night. This spirit is hidden deep in the heart of each one of us and may only emerge in silence. Even on your own at Christmas you may be less alone than somebody surrounded by people.

Each Christmas when we light our candle it is nice to remember that previous generations of our Irish ancestors have done this and that we are the custodians of our spiritual traditions and that we owe it to our descendants to pass on the real Christmas gifts that our parents entrusted to us.

Despite all the artificial glitter which sometimes seems to smother the real soul of Christmas, the beautiful reality of it will still shine forth. The first Christmas marked the coming of divine intervention to bring light and joy into our world, and because it was such a tremendous occasion, that divine coming lit a flame in all human hearts. It still glows deeply within each one of us.

Recovery Time

A S THE GLOW of Christmas fades we all feel a little bit deflated. Our weighing scales is recording higher and our bank balance lower.

But no matter what ills we inflict on ourselves, nature is always there to heal us back to wholeness. Her wide arms are opened wide to receive us and to revive our drooping spirits. Even though the countryside in winter is bleak and barren, there is still beauty in the dark gaunt branches of the leafless trees stretched heavenwards. As you walk along the country roads, they man the ditches like a guard of honour, and when the wind whips through them they wave in cheery salute. Sometimes they groan like arthritic old women when their strong knee joints are strained with the prevailing wind. If you sit on a ditch and lean against a tree trunk, you can feel the roots move beneath you. It makes you realise that a tree is a vibrant living thing which seems to be striving to push you off the ditch because you are sitting on her toes. If you ease some of the old moss off her trunk, dozens of little mites will scurry for cover. She is a host mother to a teeming hidden life.

In the autumn of '93 I collected acorns in a nearby wood and planted them in little pots in the back yard. It was wonderful in the spring to see them push their tentative heads up through the muddy brown earth. During the summer they grew stronger and thrust out small twigs with tiny green leaves that turned golden yellow in autumn. Now they are bare, frail miniature versions of their huge mother in the wood down the road. At the moment all are dormant, regenerating their regrowth beneath the earth. The trees in winter are like a government in opposition. It is a time of recovery and preparation. During this time some of the lighter twigs crack and fall to the ground in windy conditions, and occasionally a big branch will come down in a bad storm. By the end of the winter season all the weak branches and dead wood will be gone and there will be a vibrant new growth. The vineyard is being pruned.

Pruning is necessary in all worlds and a few years ago it came into mine. For a long time, behind my back door a garden grew with free abandon and flexed its muscles in all directions. It was a mini jungle where the birds built their nests, the dogs played and I went to sit and recharge my batteries when I needed resuscitation. Sometimes on these occasions I would cast my eye over the wilderness and say to the wild growth at large, "Some day I will get around to you."

During those free growing years a gardening friend would come and look around in despair and complain, "You have wonderful soil here, rich dark earth. Pity to have it wasted on you. I have clay soil and would give my eye teeth for soil like this."

She would then shake her head in frustration at the unfairness of life. She obviously did not have a father like mine who told us daily that life was unfair and the faster that we accepted that fact the better for ourselves! I tried to justify the condition of my garden by telling her that it was my thinking place and that it kept me sane. She looked at me in a strange way, and I knew that she doubted if my garden succeeded in doing even that.

But during all those years a sleeping gardener awaited awakening. This year it happened! I awoke from my slumbers and moved into the garden where I apologised to overgrown shrubs as I trimmed their abundant tresses. Trees with long skirts that trailed the ground like Victorian ladies lost their modesty at the hands of my pruner and displayed well turned ankles. Overgrown hedges got a short back and sides. I felt like the Rev. Mother in school when she swept into the room and we all straightened ourselves up and stood to attention. As I looked around the garden at the strewn limbs, I marvelled at the power of the pruner. Then I had a little conversation with myself: "Take it easy now, Alice, and don't let this power go to your head."

But I felt that my garden was breathing more freely and light was coming into corners that had never previously seen the day. An old rose bed was tidied up, and all of a sudden I became conscious of edgings. I lectured my husband on the need for tidy edges. He, who had cut the lawn during all those years of apathy, protested: "I'm cutting this lawn all my life and nobody mentioned edges. Now all of a sudden the main topic of conversation are edgings!"

A gardening partnership could break up years of happy togetherness! Nevertheless we set out demarcation lines. I kept off the grass and he kept out of the beds. We uneasily shared the edgings.

The problem of maintaining the edgings was solved, however, when a friend knocked down an old stone shed and offered us large flat stones. They became the boundary line between beds and grass. They blended in beautifully with the old stone walls of the garden and a harmonious relationship was restored.

Now that it is winter my garden is resting, but it is still providing pleasure. The bright flowers of summer are gone, but now evergreen winter shrubs that were obliterated by their flashy summer companions are coming into their own. The back benches where some of these quiet shrubs had hung back modestly during the summer are now shining forth

But the real glory of the garden at this time of the year is the birds. They are the winter flowers. Hanging off most of the trees is a bird feeder and watching them swoop in and jockey for space is one of the joys of a winter's day. Some of the feeders are outside the back windows, and many an idle minute is made enjoyable in watching their antics. If you want live theatre in your own back yard, buy a bird feeder. When I was a child and we fed the hens, the birds came in flocks for feeding. But now as methods of farming have changed many sources of food are cut off from our winter birds. In return for being fed they will give many moments of amusements, and you will discover how like ourselves they are, especially when they fight for possession.

So while the world of nature, like the Dáil, is in recess, there is still activity going on underground, and one of these days telltale signs will start to appear. Maybe I should imitate nature and use these quiet times to restore and rejuvenate my inner spirits, to sit by the fire during these long nights and catch up on my reading or maybe just to look into the fire and take time to think.

Thinking time was part of a slower way of life; now we have to make space to allow ourselves that luxury. When the new growth starts we too will spring into action if we are well rested.

A Memory Flower

IT GREW ALONG the top of a stone ditch that divided my mother's garden from the open fields. It was in every garden and self seeded, so it spread itself about with free abandon.

She called it her sweet rocket. That name seemed to suit it better than its official title, *Hesperis matronalis*.

In the era prior to the garden centre, my mother and her gardening friends exchanged slips and cuttings. When a new plant arrived into our garden, it soon discovered that it was in the midst of old bed mates who had already found their way from its former home. Many of our plants were named after their generous donors, and in later life I had an identity crisis when I had to rechristen old friends because gardening companions had difficulty with my vocabulary.

Our garden ran along the front of our long, low house, and the rocket that grew on top of the front ditch was the white frothy fringe that edged our view of the open countryside. Some of it lay down and slumbered along the stones while other tall elegant members of the family stood slim and stately and swayed delicately in the summer breeze.

I sometimes wondered, when in the world of science rockets came on stream in our bid to conquer space, did some hard-nosed scientist in a moment of romantic remembrance recall his mother's garden and decide on the name rocket. After all my mother's sweet rocket also stretched heavenwards!

It filled the garden with its sweet smell, and we collected bunches of it and placed them under the Sacred Heart picture in the kitchen and in a big jam pot in the middle of the parlour table. It did not take kindly to indoor living and shortly pined for the fresh outdoors.

When in later years I became a gardener of sorts, I remembered my mother's sweet rocket and longed for its white purity and light fragrance amongst my garden centre plants. But the sweet rocket like my youth seemed to have faded away!

But one of the joys of gardening is the discovery of the unexpected, and one day in the overflowing garden of a friend a surprise awaited me. Lo and behold! There waving her lacy arms was my sweet rocket! I knelt before her in surprise and delight. My good neighbour promptly put earth encrusted fingers around the wandering leg of Miss Rocket and followed her back to her hip joint, and I came home with my rocket trailing from my fingers. I welcomed her into my garden like a friend of my childhood. She knew that she was loved and appreciated because she settled down happily and stretched herself out. Now every morning she salutes me when I come in the garden gate, and in the evening when I rest my weary bones beside her, she fills the air around me with her heavenly essence and soothing presence. A garden must please the nose as well as the eye.

She is very sociable. After a few years, she has rambled around and her long slender neck is thrust forth between her more restrained bed companions. She is a flexible lady who can be straight and upright or can tilt forward and wrap around her neighbours. If the space is tight she can lie down and crawl forward and then prop herself up on her elbows. She will not conform and will not be penned down, so I think that this delicate looking lady is a revolutionary at heart. Because mine is a garden where all the plants are free to wander and do their own thing, she is in the right place. I find it difficult to explain the pleasure she has given me since her arrival into my garden.

In my garden, am I recreating a tapestry of memories? When I see Miss Rocket waving her delicate hands, she brings back forgotten scenes from my mother's garden. For the same reason I love sweet williams and wall flowers.

For years I did not have tall elegant white lilies. An old neighbour of my mother's had had a garden full of them, and to me as a child they were a scene of white beauty. Then one night while out for a walk I came across a friend who was doing a bit of a garden tidy up and her lilies were having their wings clipped. I came home with a bundle under my arm, and now they are standing tall in a remote corner of the garden. They were planted without sufficient thought and are not in the ideal place, but I am afraid to move them. However, another friend has promised me a rooting later on in the year, so this time I will bring my virginal ladies closer to my own corner.

Planning a garden is like painting a picture, but the joy of this picture is that it is never finished.

Off the Shelf

SOME PEOPLE LOVE buying a new pair of shoes. They enjoy the thrill of parading around the shop in front of a revealing mirror, flexing their leg muscles. They view their fine boned or thick ankles, whichever is their lot, from front, back and sides. While all these muscular gymnastics are taking place they have eyes only for the smooth new shoes that have transformed broad feet into slick, smooth, ballerina elegance. They never spare a sympathetic glance for the old, shabby, battered companions that have seen them through many a foot-weary day. These old friends are lying disconsolately on the floor, wrinkled from the effort of restraining wayward bunions and aggressive corns. The well-moulded, toe-scuffed companions of yesterday's walkabouts are cast aside with their tongues hanging out. Their laces like a neglected dog's stringy tail trail along the floor. As a final indignity they are thrust unceremoniously into the box so recently vacated by their replacements. Lined with white paper it becomes their tissue edged coffin; journey's end.

Not all shoes however get such a speedy finish off. Some people believe in easing them out gradually. They become house shoes and then maybe gardening shoes and finally painting shoes. As painting shoes they take on a whole new appearance and become a record of their owner's house colour co-ordination.

There are people who are slow to part with old familiar objects. They throw out nothing but allow everything the continuity of wearing itself out to the end. Yesterday's overcoat becomes the dog's blanket and last year's cardigan the wrap-around for the hot water bottle. They live on the theory that everything will come in handy some day. The fact that if that day ever comes they will not be able to find the required article because it is buried beneath a varied collection with similar potential does not deter them in the least. They have never read a book on Feng Shui and do not adhere to the old Chinese belief that a cluttered house is a cluttered mind. An empty space to them is a challenge to be filled.

In life we are either old shoe or new shoe people, and come the end of the year we turn into old year or new year people. Some of us look back wistfully and remember, while others bang the door firmly on the year gone by without a backward glance and look forward with great expectations. Now we are coming to the end of a century. Many of us may look back and do a bit of stock-taking, trying to analyse what the years have brought us.

Sometimes in life we are so busy doing what we have to that we have no time to figure out what it is we really want to do. In recent years I have finally got around to doing a few things that I had wanted to do for a long time but had always put on the long finger. Or could it be that the time was not right? Maybe the Bible hit the nail on the head when it said that, "To every thing there is a season, and a time for every purpose under the heaven." In any case I decided to get a move on before senile decay set in and my potential for future development would be limited. I had passed the halfway mark!

I was a child of the forties, a teenager of the fifties, a wife and mother of the sixties and seventies, which I combined with running a business. Quietly the maturing years came and with them hopefully a certain amount of tranquillity. We grow calmer or crankier with age. I felt the need to keep an eye on the balance. As we grow older the sunshine of life cools a little, and if we grow sour as we grow old we erase the sun totally. I had no desire to live in darkness.

I eased myself out of the business world and the children eased themselves out of mine. Suddenly I had time! Beautiful glorious time! Time to take ideas off the back shelves of my mind, dust them down and have a good look at them. Stored away on one of these shelves was the hidden desire to wield a paint brush. No, not a paint brush to beautify the walls and exercise my arm in continuous mindless monotony. Nothing as mundane as that!

For years I had been a home decorator and had watched my pristine pastel walls, product of that annual madness called spring cleaning, gradually deteriorate over the year to greet Santa in their usual condition of paw marked grubiness. All that was behind me now as some to the chicks had fled the nest and the remainder had reached the point of restraining themselves from crayoning and chalking abstract art on the walls. Now it was my turn.

My creative urges were going to burst forth on canvas to be framed and hung as masterpieces on those same walls. That was the dream, but the reality was slightly different. I did not become a Van Gogh overnight, but the hours of sheer unadulterated pleasure were endless. I saw colour that I had been looking at all my life but had never really seen. My eyes opened, and gnarled trees, rusty gates and old stone houses became magic corners to be captured on canvas. I watched horses' legs with a new intensity, and light through trees became a subject of great interest. I even woke up early in the morning to watch the changing of the sky.

While painting was a recent challenge, writing had been my lifelong companion. But it was the kind of writing you do in quiet corners so that nobody takes much notice of Mother sitting up in bed late at night or early in the morning scribbling away. *Innishannon Candlelight* was the product of one of these late night vigils. This is a magazine written by the people of the parish and published every Christmas. The subject of each article is the writer's choice. It started in '84 and has become an annual event. In it we have chronicled the history of the village and the memories of people who are now themselves a memory. Old school photographs of which there might only be one copy in the parish are published to the delight of the subjects no longer in the first flush of youth. The sight of themselves as bare kneed, grinning urchins brings amused grins to the faces of sedate adults. *Innishannon Candlelight* is now part of our village life. When, however, I strayed further than the village publication and brought out a book which created a bit of a stir beyond the village boundaries, my family decided that Mother was capable of springing a few surprises.

Taking ideas off the back shelves of my mind over the last decade has proved very interesting. There are still some unopened boxes up there, and I look forward to taking them down before I become too senile to reach up.

Resurrection

URING THE WINTER I sometimes think that a squirrel could have been part of my ancestral tree, because my tendency is to go into hibernation and wish that I could curl up and go to sleep until the spring comes. The sombre countryside is slumbering under a grey coat and we are lashed by wind and rain. Winter for me is a waiting time when the earth draws within itself all its richness and presents us with the bare face of deprivation. I crawl through the cold days of January and the hope of spring sleeps deep in my frozen soul. I look out my attic window at the trees in the wood on the hill opposite and sometimes see a stark beauty in their nudity, but other times they are like black beggarmen waiting for things to come. They and I are living in the hope of better days ahead.

Then one day the first flicker of future comings fans that seed of hope into a tiny flame. I hear a bird give a special early morning chirp. The shadows drifting across the evening fields take on a warmer shade. The wood seen from a certain angle has a tinge of green. A soft mild breeze wafts over the land, and the first of the snowdrops and crocuses tentatively peep up and their vivid colours glow against the dark brown earth. It is a signal that winter is on the wane and that spring is coming to fill our days with colour.

A little bud deep in the dark recesses of our winter mind gently unfolds and we too become more alive.

On the farm when I was a child we were very conscious of

this awakening, as nothing puts the closed sign on the door of winter like the sight of newborn lambs dancing in a green field. They stir some primitive instinct within us and our hearts do a little dance with them.

At this time of year many farmers keep midnight vigils behind expectant cows. The sight of a baby calf taking its first doddering steps beneath its mother's head as she licks it dry for its new life never ceases to awaken one's wonder at nature's maternal instincts.

Mother nature wakes up slowly and gently. Deep in the bowels of the earth growth is uncoiling, and in the spring the ploughing farmer thrusts life deep into its brown depths. A man, a horse and his plough were a symbol of the ability of man and nature to sustain life from mother earth. Delicate green shoots as they appear above the brown earth are a salutation to the work of man and the existence of God.

Every gardener knows the exultation of creation. I am a recent convert to gardening and like all late converts I am full of enthusiasm and lack of knowledge. In the autumn I plant bulbs thinking that maybe they will never again be heard of, and then one day they peep up and I feel that I am a creative genius and that I will soon be taking over the gardening column in the local paper. Every day I inspect their progress and glow with pride and they make me feel that God and I together are doing a great job, though he is leaving all the dirty work to me.

Around me in the garden the birds are singing, saluting the coming of spring and heralding the joy of the resurrection. The little ones flutter between the tree branches, preparing their homes for the new life about to begin. There is joy in their song, and no matter how busy they are they still fill the air with their delight which makes me think that I should provide an audience. My garden is for listening and thinking and doing as little work as possible. I watch the big birds fly back and forth across the sky in large groups, and there is harmony in their formation

Early in the morning, if I can drag myself out of bed, I come out here and watch the mist lift off the trees and see the brightening light give different shades to the grass. The garden then is a place of huddled shapes that are all waking up and stretching themselves out from under the shadows and putting on their day clothes.To hear the dawn chorus in the spring is to feel the blood begin to warm in your veins and to feel your frozen winter bones about to thaw out. The dawn chorus is a wonderful alarm clock to the new day. It does not jolt you into wakefulness. The first sound is a faint twitter as gentle as a dewdrop on the subconscious. Slowly it grows into a soft chorus of thistledown voices that gradually lift your eyelids to the beginning of a new day. To welcome its arrival in this way is to insulate yourself against any mind battering the rest of the day might cast upon you.

Spring is preparing the countryside for new life, and no matter how far from the land we live, the very air we breathe carries the vibrant message of this season. Our world is changing from a harsh, scraggy old man into a soft, shy young girl in the first flush of youth, and out on our streets young girls are the first to shed their winter garb and dance forth in bright spring colours. They cause the male population to straighten their shoulders and put pep in their steps, awakening the romance that is buried even in the most cynical heart. This is the lubricant that oils the wheels of life and causes them to run freely rather than grind painfully along.

With the coming of St Valentine's day the little bud of spring that is deep in all our hearts flowers into a bouquet of romance. It bursts open the door into spring and bangs shut the door of winter. We are alive and kicking after a long winter and this is the first opportunity to celebrate. We see bunches of daffodils and tulips glowing at every street corner and pouring out the doors of the flower shops. They are telling us that it is an occasion for love and romance. It is time to tell the person we love that we love them, and if we are not good on words a romantic card and a gorgeous bouquet of flowers speak volumes. There is nothing to warm the cockles of the heart like flowers. I would rather be buried in flowers while I can enjoy them rather than be decked with them at my final parting.

> Give me a bunch
> Of dew fresh flowers.
> What if they will not last?
> I cannot live in the future;
> The present is all I ask.

St Valentine's day is about living and loving and celebrating life and taking the one you love out to dine, and if that is beyond your budget, a walk in the newly awakening countryside is just as romantic. I once asked an old neighbour how he was and he answered, "Good, and when you are good you should say that you are good."

Now as I look out my window at the wood on the hill opposite I can see stronger tinges of green in the evening light. In a few weeks time the earth beneath the branches will be covered in a carpet of bluebells. Nature is busy decorating our world and homemakers everywhere catch this contagious fever of spring cleaning.

It is a wonderful time for babies to be born because nature is celebrating its own rebirth. They are coming into a world of new beginnings, and maybe the first stimulating colour their eyes will see is the sunshine yellow of the daffodils. A sight to gladden all our hearts is a vase of golden daffodils on our kitchen table, but they are more glorious by far if they have come from your own garden or even window box. They bring the smile of spring to our tired winter faces and open our minds to the bright new world outside.

It is fitting that Easter is a spring feast. As the fallen leaves were buried in the earth for renewal, Our Lord is taken down from the cross and entrusted into the earth. He too bursts forth in the glory of resurrection, and nature celebrates this event. Because we are part of it all, let the risen joy lift us as well and let's go out there and celebrate. Sing with the birds and dance with the daffodils. It is smiling time, laughing time, loving time. It is resurrection time and it is good to be out of hibernation.

The Other Side of the Brain

T HE VOICE AT the other end of the phone was soft, seductive and infinitely persuasive.

I can never resist a man with a mastery of flowery words so I was at the mercy of this honey-voiced charmer. Before going off the phone he had extracted a promise that the article would be in the post by Monday.

God! I thought, this is a deadline. I who had grown up in a world where fields of time had stretched in all directions, the product of an era when time was of no consequence, I was now living in a world where time seems to have disappeared down a bottomless hole. I can never quite understand how it all happened.

One of my friends takes great pleasure in parading my shortcomings before my misbelieving eyes: "Alice, your problem is that you believe that tomorrow is going to be longer than today."

Maybe she is right, but it is a great excuse to put off unpleasant jobs. Anyway, whoever said that tomorrow was going to be shorter than today, though sometimes you could be forgiven for thinking that there was going to be no tomorrow if you looked for an explanation of the mad scramble that we live in. Are we all living out of the left hand side of our brains?

A few years ago I decided to cultivate the right hand side of my brain. When I informed one of my sons, he asked, "What brain?" Teenage children have the happy knack of totally annihilating Mother's self-esteem in two caustic charged words. Just as Mother is entering the sea of menopausal, middle-aged self-doubts, they hit you on the head with the edgy stone of adolescent agony. It is nature's sense of perfect timing that when you are getting out at one end of the boat they are getting in at the other end!

An old man who lived near us had as his maxim when confusion arose, "Steady the boat." It is now getting slightly more difficult to keep the boat steady. My mother never allowed storms to rock her boat and seemed to sail through life on a sea of tranquillity. She lived out of the right hand side of her brain. It definitely made a difference to the quality of our lives. When she visited my home in recent years as the children were growing up, they always welcomed her with open arms. Children love people who give them time. One of my sisters says philosophically that children go where the good times are, and watching mine in action that is very true. Children are blessed with such a sense of enjoyment that they are attracted to the fun things in life. They definitely live out of the right hand side of their brains. Daily practicalities pose no problem, and to them life is for loving and laughing.

Meeting mothers around the country at book signings, some say, "Oh the children now have everything, but they appreciate nothing." Others have a different opinion: "Didn't we have a great time when we were young. They have nothing now."

The truth is somewhere in between: they are probably no different from what we were and will have their own memories.

A few years ago I happened in on a teenage disco. Talk of a culture shock! I thought that there was a need to call the fire brigade. Dark shadowy figures swayed around in a smoky gloom with yellow and red flashing lights and thundering sound. You would need a flash lamp to check out you partner. My children assured me that the generation gap led to my lack of understanding.

I discovered too late in life that the secret of peace in a house of teenagers was a shut mouth. Not their mouths but mine! It would have spared me endless hours of futile arguments if I had made that discovery as a young mother determined to rear model children. It took me years to learn what my mother knew instinctively. I had no excuse for not getting it right, because all I had to do was to give a repeat performance. So maybe my son was right when he queried, "What brain?"

The one thing to be said about teenagers in the house is that life is never dull. They accept no sacred cows and dig up our complacency until we feel the draught. They keep the brain sharp and our minds active and if you let it happen they will give you no life of your own. But this is where natural selfishness comes to the rescue. Teenagers are no respecters of martyred mothers.

Many interesting letters come my way and one that came this morning brought a howl of amusement from my disrespectful family. A group in another county were having a "Celebrity Auction" for charity and requested an item of personal belongings to be auctioned. One of my bright sparks suggested a frilly panties, while another decided that a long legged, pink knickers would be more reminiscent of my era.

But to get back to the right hand side of the brain, I decided to develop it a few years ago as a result of reading a book called *Storytelling, Imagination and Faith*. It tells of developing our creative side which lies dormant in most of us, waiting to be stirred into action.

When all my children have fled the nest, I have no plan to join the work force and add to the confusion already out there. I plan to retreat to a small stone house on the side of a hill and in winter to toast by a turf fire and drink hot punch. In the summer I will sleep out in the wood and listen to the dawn chorus and the wood waking up. I will write and paint and develop the right hand side of my brain and turn into a weird old lady.

Around the Bend

M Y YOUNGEST SON stood at the door of my attic room and viewed it with disdain.

"This is a dump," he declared.

The declared dump is my under-the-roof nest where I come to escape from people. I do not always succeed.

"You should get yourself a proper desk," he pronounced. "That old table covered with the red cloth trailing down to the floor cods nobody. I can see the boxes full of all sorts of rubbish bulging out through that cloth. You need a proper filing system!"

This was my holy of holies that was being attacked. My second womb! The birth place of all my books! But the desecrator of my hatching house was not yet finished.

"And that old computer," he asserted, "is an antique, completely out of date."

I was speechless. The fact that I had graduated on to a computer at all was a miracle in my eyes. I, who had been schooled on the N pen and had written my first book with the aid of a pencil and rubber! Not only had I been computer illiterate, but I had been computer terrified. I could not even type. I was away down on the ladder of progress, but if you are the mother of computer whizz kids you can find yourself taking a couple of running steps at a time up that ladder.

A few years previously, having decided that their mother needed to be introduced to the twentieth century, they had presented me with a computer. I had arrived home one night to find it glowering at me, a self-righteous, pristine presence in my shabby attic. I decided that the computer was a "he". It had a malevolent male look about it. I felt as if I were being asked to share my bed with a spaceman. His ways might not necessarily be mine! It sat there for three days while I walked around it in awe. Many years ago when I was a child, an old neighbour who had no bull brought his cows for a sexual exchange with our menacing monster, but before hostilities began a wary circling took place in order to ascertain certain facts. Something similar to that primitive exchange now took place in my attic, and I was not at all sure that I was going to enjoy the forthcoming experience.

Then one morning I woke up full of confidence and determination. Thank God for days like that! I looked at myself in the mirror.

"Taylor," I addressed myself sternly, "this is not going to beat you. You are going to teach yourself to type. The world is full of dimwits who can type."

There was no question of returning to a typing class. I had a mental block about them. Years previously I had signed on for one in the nearest town. On the second night of the course I had left home in a deluge but was assured by husband and sons that there was no question of roads' being flooded. After the class I started for home in blinding rain, and on rounding a corner of the road, a sea of water stretched ahead as far as the eye could see. As the road ran parallel to the river I could not be sure where one ended and the other began. Two lorries stood stranded in the middle of this brown swirling lake. A watery grave would not be my first choice, but my options were limited and a chance had to be taken. A terrified maniac took over. I changed gears, put my foot to the floor and got through to the other side with my hands fastened to the steering wheel in a cold clammy sweat. I never went back to that typing class.

So instead of a typing class I decided to investigate my husband's old books. He has a book on how to do most things. During our long years of marriage any hobby or new endeavour I took on board he already had a book on how to succeed at it, and so it did not surprise me when I came across A *Comprehensive Longman's Typing Book*. As old as the hills and as wise. Every day I did a lesson and after a month I was typing: not speeding, but cruising along comfortably.

One evening another son viewed my efforts.

"What are you doing with that moth eaten old book?" he demanded.

"Quite nicely," I told him icily.

"Do you know something," he told me in his best school-master's voice, "you are like someone travelling in a donkey and cart up a mountainy road while beside you is a motorway and you could be scorching along in a limo."

"How come?" I enquired

"There are disks that teach you how to type. Streets ahead of that old book. You'll learn in no time."

The following evening a disk called "Mavis Benson Teaches Typing" arrived. She was set in motion and she, who was to wave a magic wand over my typing, proved a very stern task master. When I made a mistake she said in a pained reproving voice, "That was not very good, was it? Shall we try again?" Maybe it was a clash of personalities, but after a few lessons Mavis Benson joined all the other rubbish under the red tablecloth and I was back with my old friend *Longman's*. We were two of a kind and got along well together and finally I was quite satisfied with my typing rate.

At first I continued to write everything by hand and then type it up because I could not think into the computer, but one day the big breakthrough came. Full of inspiration and enthusiasm I typed straight on to the computer. It was wonderful. A barrier had been broken. I could think into it. But disaster lay around the corner. The male monster whom I had always suspected was lying in wait to catch me out awoke from his slumbers behind the screen. I had saved as I went along, but that night when I came back up to the attic to read the entire chapter, it was nowhere to be found. The monster had eaten it! I was assured by a computer-wise son that such a thing could not happen. But I knew better, because it had happened.

"What did you do?" he demanded.

"Exactly what you told me."

"If you did, it would be here."

"I knew I couldn't trust that thing," I cried, "and that was the best piece I ever wrote and now it has gone."

"Go away," he told me, "and give me a chance to sort it out. If you saved it, it must be here somewhere."

I stomped down the stairs swearing vengeance on the computer and full of regrets for my old pencil and pad. If you lost a page of the pad, you would always find it under the bed or somewhere around the house. The best thing that I had ever written and now nowhere to be seen! Because it was gone, it was getting better by the minute. I slapped saucepans around the kitchen in angry frustration.

Ten minutes later a triumphant head appeared around the kitchen door. "I found it," he declared.

"You're a genius," I told him maganimously, all my previous annoyance evaporating.

"Wish I could return the compliment."

My computer and myself built up a rocky relationship built on mistrust. I was convinced that in its depths was a little man waiting for me to slip up so that he could pull a fast one on me. I never gave him a chance. Gradually I learned that if I treated him with respect he never let me down. An understanding grew between us. Our relationship deepened and love blossomed. There was no way now that I would part with him for a more up-to-date model. I was not going to take my son's advice on that one; but maybe he was right about the desk and the filing. Boxes under the table are not the ideal filing system. I spent much of my time in the kneeling position with my head under the table, groping around in the twilight zone looking for lost notes. The situation could be improved! But I did not want a modern streamlined desk; it could block my thinking and upset the spirit of my room.

By one of those strange coincidences that sometimes happen in life, a furniture catalogue arrived in the post the following week. I love all kinds of catalogues: gardening, clothes, electric equipment. I could browse for hours imagining many possibilities – my garden transformed with all types of exotic plants, my body made beautiful with elegant clothes – but unfortunately for the people who send out these catalogues, as soon as I put them down I forget all about my grandiose plans.

This time was different. There, staring me in the face, was just the right desk for my attic. It had a high back with drawers overhead and underneath it was a little timber filing cabinet on wheels. What I liked most about it was that it did not look like a desk. It looked more like a press. On reading all the details I decided that the man who designed it must have had me in mind. It was my dream come true! The only fly in the ointment was measurements, which the catalogue gave. The stairs up to my attic are very narrow, with a severe right hand bend. Would my dream desk make it round the bend? I got out my tape and measured my bend. I calculated that it should just barely make it round that bend, with a bit of luck and a few prayers. I did not risk asking my male advisers to measure in case I would be told that it was out of the question. I did not want to hear any negative opinions, and some of my sons have never heard about the power of positive thinking.

I rang the store that stocked the desk. The price made me swallow hard a few times, but my grandmother had always told me that you had to pay for quality. When I placed my order, they informed me that my desk should be with me in about six weeks. The week before the new arrival was due I cleaned out the attic. At a previous time the low ceiling had been papered, but in the intervening years the corners of each roll had crinkled and now they trailed down like the drooping wings of sick hens. I decided that I would pull off the bits that were trailing down. The corners, however, had no intention of being separated from the main body, so once I started to pull, the whole thing came down on top of me, bringing a shower of old ceiling-white chippings with it. The resulting ceiling looked quite interesting. In today's world of interior design we hear quite a lot about achieving the distressed look. I had it with no effort whatsoever on my part. I dragged a large bucket of white emulsion up the stairs and painted everything. The ceiling slopes to meet the walls, so it is difficult to know where one finishes and the other begins. I slobbered the thick white emulsion into all the cracks, and when I was finished the whole room looked like a hill field after a snowstorm. I was now ready to receive my desk. I was really looking forward to its arrival, but pushed away back at the far reaches of my mind was a tiny seed of apprehension about its making it around the bend.

On a mellow September day the store rang to say that the delivery van was on its way. I was at the door to welcome my new working companion. Two cheery delivery men eased it out of the van and into the front hallway, where they stripped it of its corrugated paper wrapping. I stood back to admire the new desk. It was definitely a "she". Fine boned and elegant she was, just as I had imagined her. I ran my fingers lovingly over her beautiful soft texture and opened her drawers to sniff her rich woody smell. The two delivery men waited patiently for instructions.

"Up two flights of stairs," I told them apologetically.

"That's no bother," one of them assured me pleasantly.

"Well the first one will be no bother," I told him, "but the second one might be."

"Why?" he asked

"Well," I admitted reluctantly, "there's a bend."

"You think that it might not go around it?" he asked worriedly.

"If it doesn't," I told him, "I'm going to have a nervous breakdown!"

I led them up the first stairs, which as I had anticipated posed no problem, and then we arrived at the foot of the next stairs. The delivery man eyed it warily but after walking up and down a few times decided, "We might just about make it."

I sighed with relief. But the relief was short lived, because my lovely desk, despite much coaxing, did not quite make it around that bend. My two gallant men tried her from another angle, and then another angle, but she was just too leggy. One of them looked at me sympathetically, "I think, Missus, that it's time for that nervous breakdown," he told me.

"It won't fit?" I asked sadly.

"Not a hope," he assured me. "We'll take it back."

"No, don't take it back," I told him. "Let it stay there."

"It's your call, Missus," he told me, "but I can't see you making it around that bend."

"We'll see," I told him, "and I'll get back on to you tomorrow if it's to be collected."

"Grand job," he told me happily and went down the stairs whistling, glad to be rid of me and my bend.

I had no immediate solution to the problem, but I felt that the two delivery men were from modern semi-detached houses in suburbia where the geography was square and uncomplicated and they knew nothing about the spinal curvature of old houses. My old house is a modern architect's nightmare because nothing is quite as it should be: walls are not straight, corridors change their mind and turn sharply in another direction, floors are not level and when you walk over some of them they groan in protest. I understand this old house and know that sometimes it can be awkward, but then for no specific reason it could decide to co-operate. It all depended on how it was feeling on the day. I hoped and prayed that this was a good day!

I summoned son number one to the rescue. He is the one that I would send for if I were stranded on a desert island because he would be sure to arrive. He sized up my desk, peered up the stairs at the bend, looked at me and demanded, "Did you measure before you ordered?"

"Well, I kind of did," I murmured.

"Huh," was his only comment.

"This is what we'll do," he instructed. "You go up ahead and pull and try to angle it sideways, and I'll lift from the back."

I did as instructed. I tried to angle her but she was not very flexible and her high shoulder dug into the wall. I pulled and he pushed, but there was no way that my lady's elegant shoulder was going to make it around that bend. An inch less and we would have been home and dry! Maybe if we got it from another angle I thought.

"Take her down again," I called from above.

"My bloody back is cracking under her," came from below.

But down she went again. We tried another angle and she came a bit further, but then she wedged.

"She's stuck," I said in alarm. "She won't come up or down."

"We're rightly shagged now," came from below, and I made a quick decision that it was no time for correcting bad language. As the desk completely blocked the stairs I could not see my first born, but I knew from the tone of voice that he was under pressure. So was I, and my lovely desk was stuck at a most unladylike angle with her legs in the air.

"What the hell is going on?" Another son had arrived.

"Your mother's bloody desk won't go up this fecking stairs."

I was being disowned by the eldest brother and was now only the mother of the next one, who was not going to let a golden opportunity pass him by.

"That would do grand in my room," the opportunist announced.

"Shut up," he was told by two of us. At least we agreed on one thing.

"Some of that dividing partition to the next attic will have to come down to get her up," he declared, and before I could protest his brother agreed with him.

"Jesus," I wailed, and I did not know if it was a prayer or a protestation, but maybe the man Himself would decide.

A hammer arrived on the scene. After a few well-aimed belts the adjoining slab and plaster partition crumbled and a shower of dust and plaster poured down on my new carpet and over my elegant desk, but at least her high shoulder sank thankfully into the newly made black hole.

"Now," a voice from below instructed, "we'll try again."

She came a little further up, but then she hit an upright cross beam.

"Jesus!" I wailed again.

A son's head appeared between the desk and the wall and a hand shook the cross beam.

"I wonder could we move this?"

"No, no," the other son shouted in alarm, "it's connected to the main joist of the house. The roof will fall in!"

"Oh, my God," I groaned.

"Take away more of the partition," came the instruction. "Maybe if we got her more upright before the bend we'd get around it."

So more plaster poured down, my carpet disappeared from view under a thick fog and the desk was shrouded in a grey cloak. We tried again but to no avail.

"It's no good, " came the joint decision from below.

"Take her down and we'll think it out again," I instructed, spitting bits of mortar out of my mouth.

The desk thumped down the steps of the stairs and I came after it. My two dust-covered sons stared at me balefully.

"There is one thing for certain anyway," the eldest said decisively, "you can't send it back now, and the other certainty is that it won't go up to your attic."

"Don't you open your mouth about it going into your room," I threatened the other one.

"I didn't say a word," he protested.

"Yeah, but I know what you're thinking."

"There is no law against thinking, and anyway where's it going to go?"

"Up to my attic."

"Can't be done."

Into this scene of turmoil, dust and confusion, my husband arrived and his eyes widened in amazement when he viewed the desk, the hole in the wall and his bedraggled warring family.

"It won't go around the bend, " he said evenly, choosing his words carefully.

"No," son number two declared, "and your wife is driving us around the bend."

My maternal role was gradually being eroded. I was going to finish up being nobody's mother.

"We are all going down to the kitchen to have something to eat," I decided, before I took the hammer to my two sons. "My grandmother always said that you should eat in times of stress."

"Did your grandmother ever tell you that is was a good thing to know when your beaten?"

"No," I told my eldest son, "she always said that you can if you think you can."

"That explains a lot," he concluded.

We retired to the kitchen where the kettle was put on and tea was made, and gradually we recovered our equilibrium or at least some of it.

"There is only one solution to the problem," my husband announced.

"What?" we chorused.

"I will take it apart and reassemble it in the attic."

"Oh my God, " I groaned silently, "why is this happening to me?"

The ache that had been confined to my head for the previous two hours now crashed into the rest of my body. It was as if my own limbs were about to be dismembered and reassembled in the attic.

"Will it come back together?" I asked weakly.

"We'll see," I was told evenly.

All of a sudden my sons discovered that they all had other pressing jobs that needed attention. They were abandoning the sinking ship! My husband and I returned to the scene of destruction at the foot of the attic stairs. Like a surgeon about to perform a major operation, he collected his tools. But this was more of an autopsy, because an entire body had to be taken apart and reassembled.

I felt that the following hours were going to sorely test my marriage of many years. The first thing I prayed for was silence, which has never been one of my strong points, but I sensed that the wrong word could be fatal for the patient. This patient was well put together. Her joints were screwed, dowelled and glued. The craftsman who had put her together had meant her to stay that way. When her right hand side was eased away from the main body, I felt as if my right hip were being eased out of its socket. I said a silent prayer when the dowels did not crack. Slowly and painfully she came apart while beads of perspiration gathered on my husband's forehead. A stream of stress ran down my back as I carried the separated limbs up the stairs. Finally she was laid out on the attic floor. She had come apart but would she go back together again?

My husband picked up her back panel and I raised her right hand side. With wordless concentration we interlocked her corners. I held both together while my husband eased on her left hand side. While I stretched my arms around her to hold her together, he glued and screwed and eventually she was firm enough to be able to stand on her own two feet. With silent concentration we laboriously eased on her other vital statistics, and very very slowly she began to take shape. I started to breathe more freely. As each of her joints was firmed together the pain left mine, and when she stood complete and as good as new, all my pains and tensions evaporated. With relief came exhaustion, and as it was the middle of the night we fell into bed.

The following morning, as soon as I woke, I jumped out of bed and ran up the attic stairs to view my desk. It looked perfect, quite at home in the corner of the attic, where it fitted snugly under the sloping roof. All the effort had been worth while. The rest of the morning was spent reslabbing and plastering the damaged wall, and by lunch time it was ready for painting, and all the dust and dry plaster had been hoovered up.

My sons were impressed in spite of themselves. They had to admit that you would never think that she had been taken asunder to come around the bend!

"Should you ever decide to move it," my youngest threatened, "we'll take off the roof."

House Coats

"WHY DID YOU paint your house knickers-pink?" my best friend demanded.

"What do you mean by knickers-pink?" I protested.

"Well," she informed me, "when I was young my grandmother always put her washed knickers on the laurel hedge to dry, and they were always that colour. Since then whenever I see that colour I think of my grandmother's knickers."

I looked at her in dismay but she was in full flight and wanted to elaborate on her theme. "As a matter of fact," she continued, "every knickers in the country was that colour at the time. So your house will bring back memories of old knickers to everyone who looks at it."

She confirmed my worst fears. My house was a terrible colour! What had appeared on the colour chart as "old rose" had turned into a "changeling" on my big rambling house. If mine had been a small, well-designed house tucked away discreetly in a back street, it might not have mattered very much. But there I was, right on the corner, in the heart of our little village, a big, vulgar, pink powder puff of a house. I had got it wrong! I, who had ambitions for our village to do well in Tidy Towns. Our only hope now was if the adjudicator was colour blind or had happy childhood memories of the Pink Panther.

I tried to convince myself that it was not so bad, but a romantic friend who loved happy-ever-after books told me dreamily, "Your house is beautiful! It reminds me of Barbara Cartland."

My young daughter was not so romantic: "Ours is the yuckiest house in the village," she informed me.

I lived with that terrible house colour for four years. Earlier this year my daughter announced, "We no longer have the yuckiest house in the village." She led me to an upstairs window from where we had a full view down over the village street, and there was a house that had previously settled into the background now yelling its head off in a vile pink with a sick orange door and windows. I opened my mouth to criticise and then slammed my jaw bones shut. Who was I to stand in judgement, I who had painted my house in memory of my grandmother's knickers?

That day I decided that enough was enough! I rang the painter and told him to drop in some charts, that we were going to paint the house. Then the mind churning began. On such occasions, family are worse than useless. They can all tell you what is wrong but have no alternative suggestions. I got dark threats of "For God's sake, get it right this time," but with no guidelines as to how to go about it. The painter suggested a colour, telling me that it was on a house in the next village. I went to have a look. The house screamed down the village street at me in a veil of purple rage. The painter was the same man who had put my grandmother's pink knickers on four years previously, so he was not much better than myself.

I decided that a whole new approach was in order. We were going to leave the world of pink and red behind and go blue. I am not a blue person, but a friend with colour co-ordination experience had come to my rescue just as I was about to get a colour breakdown. She suggested a deep blue, which left me cold, but she suggested teaming it with a poppy red door. I fell for the poppy red door. I have always loved doors that make a statement. Bright vivid doors that say welcome. Now at last I was to have one!

The painter was delighted with my choice. That made me nervous.

"I have always wanted to try that colour match," he told me, "but no one would chance it."

That made me more nervous.

"Don't lose your nerve," my sister advised over the phone. "The secret of changing your house colour is not to lose your nerve at the last minute, especially when the house is half the old colour and half the new colour."

When the house was in such a condition the school children on the way home that evening all went, "Ooh, ooh, ooh, isn't it horrid." But I held my nerve! I was beginning to see light at the end of the tunnel. I believed that the poppy red door would bring it all together. As my front door was transformed into a scarlet lady, I held my breath in delight at the colour contrast, until a neighbour from up the hill came to a standstill in front of it with look of profound shock on her face.

"You're surely not going to let the door that colour?" she protested.

But I was not to be put down. I had a vision of the final picture in my mind and I had the scent of success in my nostrils. This time my colour was going to be beautiful! The front door was such a success that I viewed the side door with a wicked gleam in my eye. Years previously in a moment of extreme bad taste, I had installed a plastic side door to which I had taken an instant dislike. Now I decided that my hour had come and that a bright red coat would transform this insipid, frigid, flat-chested lady into an flamboyant Botticelli-like welcoming hostess. The painter had reservations. "Never painted a plastic door before," he told me.

"Always a first time," I replied airily. I was on a good run and I was not going to lose my nerve now. The red coat did wonders for my plastic door and eradicated my moment of bad taste from years previously. The window sills became pristine white, and the evening that I placed the window boxes of bright red geraniums on them the whole house jelled together.

The dark blue walls stood with dignity on the village corner and the bright happy flowers winked conspiratorially at the poppy red doors. The rambling house was like an elegant old lady dressed up for a wedding. Nobody would know that beneath all her finery she was wearing her grandmother's pink knickers.

It Runs in the Family

I T IS LATE August in Ballybunion and a warm clinging mist is drifting in from the sea. It wraps itself like a moist shawl around my head. We came late last evening. I love this place: the feel of the sand beneath my feet, the smell of the seaweed and the droning sound of the sea. I usually spend a week here, but this year I have only two days so every moment is precious.

The beach is quiet now as all the people have gone back up into the town. I like it best at this time. I like to walk around the Castle Green, out through the doorway in the old castle and look down at the waves swirling against the rocks below; to look away out to sea and see the lighthouse winking across the water. I lean over the railings, and the serenity of the shimmering sheet of water washes over me.

Then I scramble down the side of the hill and across the Women's Strand. It is still called the Women's Strand, the name a relic of another era of separate bathing areas. There is nobody swimming. The sea is resting peacefully, drifting over the ruffled sand and soothing it after the turmoil of the day. Sand castles are levelled and footprints wiped away. As it smooths the sand it soothes my mind.

I walk past Mary Collins' seaweed baths where everything is tidied away after the day. A row of multi-coloured bath towels sway in the breeze. The little blue tea room is locked up and the shop shutters are bolted down. A red bucket and spade are sheltering in a corner, waiting for their forgetful owner to return in the morning.

I climb up the steep steps to the other headland. Since last year the hilltop path has been improved. I regret the change. It takes away some of the natural country feel of the place and gives it the look of a planned walk. Maybe it had to be made safe. From this high vantage I can look down over the strands and watch the tide gradually cover the Black Rocks. As a child I often feared getting trapped on those rocks and being surrounded by sea. The setting sun is making holes in the curtain of mist and Clare is coming and going in the distance.

As I approach the Nine Daughters' Hole I feel the old sense of foreboding. The sound of the sea pounding against the rocks below and the eerie hollow thud as it forces itself through the gaping rock face send chills down my spine. Because I am on my own I creep in close to the edge and cautiously peer down. I am fascinated and repelled. When there is anybody with me, I never go near the edge in case they might topple in. Now I am only responsible for myself so I enjoy giving myself the shivers. I am glad and regretful to leave it behind.

With a sense of anticipation I reach the path above the Nun's Strand and look down. The sudsy sea is rolling in along the yellow tongue of sand and the white foam is swirling around the black legs of the Virgin Rock. If my eleven-year-old daughter had been with me I would have been persuaded to clamber down through the Smugglers' Cave, but she is up at the Merries having a rip roaring time with the bumpers and slot machines, so I am free to sit on a soft tuft of grass with my back to the convent wall and watch the sea. The mist has obliterated Clare and is curling up the back of Virgin Rock.

Later I call to the Merries to collect her. I am persuaded to stay on and she drains my pockets of available money, which she pumps into the gaping mouths of flashing machines. She dances in anticipation in front of them, hoping that they will cough up a fortune, and then groans in frustration when the steel monster proves too smart for her.

I watch the other families: patient countrymen smiling indulgently at excited children; harassed mothers trying to keep track of a wandering brood. Against my better judgement I am coaxed into bingo by a conniving daughter. I am not a bingo person, and as the numbers are called my mind wanders and I forget about the job on hand. An irate daughter slaps the little plastic doors across my bingo numbers. She rolls her eyes to heaven at the affliction of a mother who is not smart enough to play bingo. Some daughters have a lot to put up with!

Leaving the bingo behind the nightly visit for burger and chips is observed. I get indigestion just watching her polish off this load of junk. We sit on the wall of the old Tricky Tracky shop where she savours her feast. I am offered one tomato sauce covered chip which I eat against my better judgement.

Teenagers walk past laughing and singing. Some chase each other around cars and hurl irreverent insults back and forth. From her vantage point on the wall, she views them with curiosity. In a few years she will be one of them.

Every summer she has come here and it is the highlight of her year. I am glad of all the times that we have spent here together. Will she, I wonder, bring her children back here as I have brought mine? If she does, she will be the fifth generation of our family to make this place part of their lives. Ballybunion runs in our family.

Faces of Cork

O N A FEW occasions in life you dance in harmony with your own place. These moments are pictures that hang along the walls of your memory. An occasion that enshrined for me the sense and soul of Cork was the funeral of Br Matthew, a Franciscan friar from Liberty St. The Poor Clares and the Franciscans are the comforters to whom the people of Cork turn in time of crisis. Over the years many troubled souls had found in Br Matthew a sympathetic ear and a giving hand. The day he died they came to say thanks and brought the soul of Cork with them.

That night a line of people moved slowly up the side aisle of St Francis' Church, past the coffin in the friars' private chapel where Br Matthew's body lay in his brown Franciscan habit. These people told the story of the life of Matthew and the essence of Cork. They spanned the divide from those who had made it to the top to those who had never got past the bottom, and it was one of the latter who told the most interesting story.

A battered middle-aged man whose face was a record of long years dedicated to a great thirst shook his head with regret and said, "When I was too pissed to go home he called to the mother and kept her company, and since she died he never forgot her anniversary." Then he shook his head sadly. "I'll have no one to talk to now that he's gone."

A little old lady wrapped in a tight grey coat that clung to her childlike figure shuffled along in a pair of large floppy bedroom slippers, supported by a tiny walking aid with a white plastic bag hanging off the bars. Beneath a black cloche hat pulled well down over her face, a pair of bright inquisitive darted out at me.

"I knew him since he was a boy," she declared.

She had lived in a room in one of the narrow streets behind the friary, and he had helped to get her a Share house – a comfortable home provided by the students of Cork for the elderly.

Another old lady sobbed into a tattered tissue in the back pew.

"Ah Matthew," she sighed, "he was one of the best. I sometimes found it hard to manage, and he helped me to pay my rent."

They mourned him because he had brought brightness into dark days.

In his homily at the funeral mass the celebrating friar said, "Br Matthew's world knew no boundaries; to him all people had goodness in them."

He continued to tell that when at night they had to ask the winos and down-and-outs to leave the church so that they could lock up, Br Matthew had always requested, "Be nice to them."

As we walked down the aisle behind his coffin, a stranger and I chatted. "He knew everybody around the city," she said, "and brought money from the well-off to those who needed it. He used to say that he was a great beggar. He was a one-man social welfare system."

He had come from the country, and weather-beaten country faces mourned him too. Men who had parked their cars around St Frances' while their wives shopped had been chatted to by this warm-hearted, interested man, who had often finished up tracing their family tree with them. He could be found in back-street pubs keeping in touch with people who had few friends.

He was himself one of a large family, who flocked to his

final celebration. Good-looking women and dark, attractive men whose faces lent themselves easier to laughter than tears now laughed and cried as they spoke of him. One sister-in-law remarked, "He visited us all but never mentioned in any house what went on in the others, and if any of our young ones stepped out of line he was in no way critical, only did all he could to help. Matt was a real peacemaker and the vine who kept us all together."

As we stood by his grave one of his fellow friars said regretfully, "There is a great richness gone with Matthew; he loved beautiful things and spread them around."

So we laid him to rest in St Finbar's cemetery, this seemingly simple man who during his life had got the Freedom of the City of Cork. A city that could acknowledge the greatness of one so simple is a city with an appreciation of its own people, a place with a royal heart and the common touch.

Another occasion that brought me close to the soul of Cork was in a bookshop. He sat in the front row, a neat little parcel of a man whose ankles were so tightly crossed that his shining brown boots appeared as one and his arms so firmly wrapped across his chest that he looked as if he wanted to take up the minimum of space. His tight navy suit did not quit reach his wrists or ankles, and under his brown felt hat a small determined chin shot out and a pair of piercing blue eyes sized me up. He stared for a long time, occasionally pursing his lips together and shaking his head. He did not appear to like what he saw.

It was my first reading in a Cork bookshop, and I was so nervous that my clammy hands clung to the page before I had even begun. Most of the people smiled encouragingly as they filed in, but I was mesmerised by the little man directly in front of me. If I had put out my hand I could have touched him, but that was the last thing that I felt like doing. Judging by the look on his face, it would not have been his first choice either.

The people were all settled in their seats waiting expectantly. The bookshop manager hovered in the background, wondering what was the delay. The little man rubbed his shoes together and twitched his nose in annoyance. There was no choice; I simply had to begin. After a stuttering start the reading got underway, and as it continued the rest of the people faded into the background and there was only me and the little man.

I wanted to please him, to bring a smile of approval to his face, but after the first paragraph I knew that success was not mine. His expression became more crucified and his lips disappeared into his mouth. I dragged my eyes from him and met the eyes of a happy faced woman in the third row, and I clung to her like a drowning victim.

When I looked at the little man again his eyes were closed. I might have thought that he had fallen asleep, but sleeping faces are relaxed and his was screwed up in agony. I determined to keep my eyes firmly averted from him, but he was like a magnet drawing my gaze back. As the reading continued his face became even more tortured.

When the reading finally finished he was obscured from view by people gathering around the table to get books signed. Then a large lady loomed over me, and sheltered beneath her overhanging bosom like a boat in harbour was the little man.

"My Jack is only weak for you," she boomed, tapping the top of the brown felt hat. "He's read all your books and thinks they're only gorgeous."

"Does he?" I gasped weakly

"He does," she pronounced; "enjoys every word of 'em."

Jack's face was a total contradiction of the word enjoyment and with every utterance by his wife his expression became more irate. I decided it was time to crack Jack's silence.

"You enjoyed them?" I enquired feebly.

"I nearly kilt meself laughing," he told me fiercely, without a smile on his face, and driving his hands into his pocket he bolted out the door.

"I Live Here"

I T WAS A Sunday in March '89 and I was on my way home by train from Dublin. I thought back over the activities packed into the weekend. My husband and I had flown from a rain soaked Cork airport to a sunny London to attend the Irish Book Fair. I had enjoyed reading to the Irish emigrants who had obviously identified closely with *To School through the Fields*. The following day I did an early morning radio interview before flying back to Dublin, where I was the guest speaker at the Book Sellers' Dinner. My first after dinner speech and I was petrified! It has been a source of amazement to me that it is assumed, because you publish a book, that you can then do other things that have absolutely nothing to do with writing.

When we arrived in Cork one of our sons, together with our ten-year-old daughter, was waiting to pick us up. While driving home they filled us in on what had been happening in our absence. I am one of these people who always feel that while I am missing a lot could have happened, which is almost never the case. Going in the door I felt the house reach out to me. I was glad to be home.

As we were having tea in the kitchen another son drifted in and said, "There was a phone call for you from an Ann McCabe in RTÉ. Something about doing a programme. She produces 'Check Up'."

"But that's a medical programme," I said. "Do they think there's something wrong with me?"

"They probably do," he was delighted to tell me, "but it's not in connection with 'Check Up' but 'I Live Here' which she also produces."

My first reaction was one of apprehension, as if someone had asked if they could come inside my head.

After the tea I went up stairs to my attic office. I needed to unroll my mind after the last few days, but it was difficult to relax as I considered the prospect of a television programme. What exactly was involved? How did I really feel about it? Did I want cameras peering into my life? And what on earth would they find to make a whole programme about? To me my life at home was so ordinary that I could not visualise it making interesting viewing for a full hour. Speaking to Ann McCabe on the phone the following day, I said just that, to which she replied, "That's exactly what we want: ordinary living."

It was decided that she would come to Innishannon and we would discuss the matter. I suppose we all have our pre-conceived notions of what people in different walks of life look like. Ann McCabe was definitely not my idea of a TV producer. Maybe I was expecting a brisk, efficient, high powered lady. Ann McCabe, however, was relaxed and happy faced, with a bubbling personality and laughing eyes. She was what my grandmother would have termed a slip of a girl. She obviously enjoyed her work and you felt that working with her would be a happy experience. After a long chat up in the attic, I decided to make "I Live Here". She smiled and said, "If we had a camera here this evening half the programme would be in the can."

That weekend as we walked around the woods and roads of Innishannon, she outlined what she had in mind and I filled her in on what was available. She made another trip south the following week to finalise the arrangements, and I showed her my old school, a little cottage called Tig Noni and the home farm in North Cork. Ann met the entire family, including my mother, and everybody felt that RTÉ in the person of Ann McCabe was not going to put undue pressure on anybody.

The last two weeks in April were set aside for the filming. I felt that Innishannon would have looked better later in the year when the woods would have donned their more colourful coats, but the big wheel that is RTÉ cannot be turned by the colour of leaves. Glorious sunshine, however, came our way as we began filming down at the old school.

It was a strange experience to see a TV crew at work in the overgrown grass around the ruins of my old school. At the same time, I was glad that they were recording a way of life that had been experienced by so many children of rural Ireland. Ken Fogarthy, the cameraman, had to perch high at a precarious angle on top of a crumbling wall to get a good shot of the old dry toilets. Those relics of our childhood would cause modern mothers to recoil in horror!

The three children dressed up to recreate a scene from those days asked how we could have possibly run barefoot across the fields. The crew worked patiently and painstakingly with the children. Anna Ryan's application to detail smoothed the way forward and the soft spoken soundman, Jim Wylde, moved around silently. The birds, as if aware that they were being recorded, sang their hearts out on top of every tree.

Getting down into the glaise where we had played on the way home from school caused great amusement. As sure footed country children we had been like mountain goats. The attempt by adults to get filming equipment in through soft mud under overhanging trees resulted in one of the crew sliding down the slippery slope in a very undignified position. The seat of his pants told the story for the rest of the day. When awkward scenes were completed we held our breath lest John Hall would announce quietly, "Hair in the gate." We had learned quickly that this meant a retake.

The indoor scenes in Tig Noni were far less arduous, and here Dermot O'Grady in his easy methodical way angled lighting with infinite precision, as the entire crew worked in silent harmony. For those three filming days of the first week we were blessed with sunshine, though a slight haze prevented a shot of my favourite hills. I discovered the importance of light and of waiting patiently until the sun came from behind a cloud. The crew were patient and meticulous people who worked long hours with immense concentration. I decided by the end of the first week that the real stars of television were behind the cameras.

The crew went back to Dublin on Friday. I was booked to speak at a conference that Friday night and another on Saturday. I had a radio interview on Monday. All these had been arranged before the filming had come on stream.

We were delighted when the sun shone again on Tuesday morning for the filming in beautiful Shippool wood, which is my favourite corner of Innishannon. Ann McCabe directed operations with a delicate touch and Ken Fogarthy's creative eye saw interesting angles. As well as the usual crew that day, we had Eva Holmes from the RTÉ *Guide* and John Rowe from the stills department of RTÉ. In between filming takes they took photographs of Shippool wood. I was glad the Shippool was the background for these photographs.

From the wood we went to the old historic graveyard and tower in the village. Doves nest in the old tower, and I had the bright idea that a flutter of wings up through the tower would make a nice shot. Unfortunately at the time there were only a few birds in residence and instead of a flutter of wings they delivered a few well aimed blessings.

During the filming period around the village everybody was interested and helpful. The greatest excitement was created however when the crew moved in to takes scenes in our supermarket. I wondered as I watched people walk in front of the camera and block off the filming how order was going to be got out of this chaos. A more daunting experience was when they moved into our kitchen and a makeshift meal was quickly put together on the table. A reluctant family were gathered around this and were supposed to project the image of an ordinary mealtime. This was rather difficult with light, sound and camera beamed on us. We were all relieved when that was over.

We finished up on Thursday with a book signing in Easons of Cork. Some of my wonderful neighbours came in for this signing, and it was a morning of laughter and fun. People who came in just to have their book signed wondered what on earth was going on. One woman, when I told her that it was RTÉ filming, just dropped her book and ran, saying, "Holy God, let me get out of here."

It is now almost ten years since that programme was made, and many changes have come to Innishannon and to my old home. Some of the people who were in it are no longer with us, including my mother, Billy the blacksmith, Mrs Hawkins and Joe Bernard. I am glad that I decided to make "I Live Here" as it is so good to have them all on film.

Faith of our Fathers

MEMORY CAN MAKE children of us all. Rhymes that we learn when we are very young stick to our minds like cream to the inside of a jug. They come back unbidden in later life and cause a spurt of joy to shoot up in our hearts. They belong to childhood days and enshrine within us a younger more innocent edition of ourselves.

In our old school we would recite lines after the teacher, and from the sheer dint of repetition they sank into our minds never to be totally forgotten. When my father recited rhymes that he had learned at school, he would encompass me in the world of his childhood, building a bridge between the generations. I was able to walk back over that bridge into his world.

You hear a half-remembered song on the radio, and all of a sudden you are reversing down a time tunnel, as scenes long forgotten flash past and you are transported back through the years. When you come back to reality you shake your head and wonder how a few notes could open a door into your past.

We had an old neighbour, Jack, who used to sing "Far Away in Australia". He was not a singer and he always bellowed it forth with a huge grin on his face. One day last year I heard it on radio and it brought a huge grin to my face. Jack is long gone, but "Far Away in Australia" brought him alive in my mind. Somebody's favourite song will always awaken memories of them. It is a lovely way to remember a friend.

When the tape "Faith of Our Fathers" was brought out a few years ago it triggered off an avalanche of memories, some good and some bad. For a whole generation, my generation, those hymns were the drumbeat of their childhood. The tape lifted the dust sheets off old hymns and they came marching back into our lives.

Once again a nine-year-old Alice in a hand-me-down coat watched a black-robed missioner with upraised arms lifting the entire congregation in a thunderous ovation to God. These were solid country people not normally given to rapture, but the hymn "Faith of our Fathers" changed them in my eyes from ordinary mortals into God's army. We loved it and came out of that church feeling that we were more than farmers, shopkeepers and blacksmiths. We were God's people!

"Faith of our Fathers" also evoked warm Sunday evenings in the fifties spent listening to Mícheál Ó Hehir's voice vibrating out of the old wet-battery radio. As the last notes of the hymn faded, Mícheál took over from God and for the following hour we were not far from the gates of heaven.

Once a year the Eucharistic procession left our parish church and, having paraded all around the town, continued up the long, winding avenue to the local convent. The nuns would have erected an altar on top of the stone steps in front of the enormous oak door. Here we gathered at the foot of the steps for benediction. Drapes of white and yellow veils floated from the apex above the arched doorway, creating billowing clouds over the altar. The thurible puffed out incense that wafted up the imposing facade of the convent. The choir poured forth "To Jesus Heart All Burning". One year the floating veils caught fire and we nearly had to change our tune.

"Hail Queen of Heaven" brought memories of a row of teenagers garbed in the blue and white of Children of Mary. We stood outside that convent and listened to the choir sing "Hail Queen of Heaven" feeling that we were "the wanderers here below". We felt that she definitely had a motherly eye on us!

"Queen of the May" took me to a wood beside Drishane Convent where as students we picked bluebells to carry in the May procession to crown a statue of Our Lady in the grounds.

"The Bells of The Angelus" and Killarney Cathedral are forever married in my mind. Every Sunday night we had a novena to Our Lady of Perpetual Succour in that beautiful cathedral, and there we sang "The Bells of the Angelus". Listening to it on the tape, I could see the dark mosaic of Our Lady of Perpetual Succour in the shadows of the towering columns of the cathedral. I was nineteen years old then, and while I sang I was looking forward to the Rugby Club Dance that would take place later in the International Hotel.

For most of us these hymns were woven into the fabric of our lives. Apart from "Cockles and Mussels" and "The Rose of Tralee", they were probably the only songs that the whole country had in common. Then they went out of fashion, evicted on to dusty shelves behind organs in churches all over the country to be replaced by modern hymns. But like the poems we learned in school, they were imprinted on the back pages of our minds, ready to be met again as childhood companions.

The Last Chapter

How dull it is to pause, to make an end,
To rust unburnish'd, not to shine in use!
As tho' to breathe were life. Life piled on life.
Were all too little, and of one to me.

WHEN I READ this poem many years ago I admired Tennyson's old Ulysses, who was not prepared to let life come to a standstill. His body had grown old but his spirit was full of adventure. So many people grow old in spirit and often wait for their bodies to catch up.

Recently a young friend whom I had not seen for a few years came to visit. When I asked about her mother, she smiled sadly and said, "My Mum has got so old and narrow. She is obsessed with the cleanliness of the house, and she is no fun to be with any more. When she comes to visit me she gives out about my house and never relaxes. She has Dad under her thumb and is making him old with her. It is so sad to see them get old before their time. It is such a waste because they are both in good health."

As she spoke I remember reading somewhere that the tragedy of life is to die while you are still alive, and I again remembered my man in "Ulysses":

... you and I are old;
Old age hath yet his honour and his toil;

Death closes all: but something ere the end,
Some work of noble note, may yet be done,
Not unbecoming men that strove with Gods.
We are not now the strength which in old days
Moved earth and heaven; that which we are, we are;
One equal temper of heroic hearts,
Made weak by time and fate, but strong in will
To strive, to seek, to find, and not to yield.

We all hope to grow old with dignity and grace, but the reality is that many of us may reach a stage when we will no longer be masters of our own destiny. As it says in the Gospel: "I tell you solemnly, when you were young you put on your belt and walked where you liked; but when you grow old you will stretch out your hands, and somebody else will put a belt around you and take you where you would rather not go."

The old are vulnerable, and the thought of old age brings out the coward in the bravest of us.

Once while in Galway I met a charming woman whose elderly mother was dying in the local hospital. Because she told me about her mother with such love, I called to see the old lady the following day. She lay back amongst the pillow like delicate lace and her face was full of gentle kindness as she whispered, "I think that I'm a burden to my children." I took the memory of her home with me and later wrote a poem for her.

The Cobweb of Old Age

Dear gentle soul,
Do not think
You are a burden:
In your love
You conceived them
And wove them
Into the fabric
Of your life,
Giving to them

All your strength.
The tide has turned.
They are the strong,
And you have your
Delicate threads caught
In the cobweb of old age.
They would wrap you
In their strength,
Let them now,
Because you can
Give them much
Of gentleness
And the wisdom of your time.

When I was invited to visit the old people of St Martha's ward in St Finbar's Hospital, Cork, last Christmas, I wondered what the experience would be like. Maybe I had an image of a grey building and grey people in my mind. But the two vibrant and charming ladies who came to pick me up were full of enthusiasm about their patients and full of the joys of life. I concluded that wherever they were in charge there would be a buzz. I was not disappointed. Far from being grey the ward was full of light, warmth and Christmas decorations. A tall red Christmas candle rooted in the traditional turnip and surrounded by holly graced a table by a glowing fire. The residents sat around in comfortable chairs with smiles on their faces while I read poems and Christmas stories. Some faces were alive with interest while others dozed off, but everybody woke up to join in the chorus of "Come back, Paddy Reilly, to Ballyjamesduff".

The nurses moved between their chairs anticipating their needs and making sure that they were all comfortable. Some were very incapacitated but all were treated with the greatest respect. The atmosphere was one of caring and kindness. On chatting to them afterwards I discovered that they were content and happy to be there. It was a very different place from what I had expected.

Afterwards we had tea and tasty mince pies, which one of the nurses had made the previous night. As I sat having tea with the residents, I concluded that this was a place where you could live out the end of your days in peace and comfort. It was wonderful to see the bright decor of the wards, the high standard of hygiene and the great care with which the nurses treated their charges. I came away feeling that ours is a better world than I had previously thought it to be, because the way we care for the old and vulnerable of our world is surely a measure of how civilised a society we are.

The Last Chapter

Stripped of independence
By old age.
She lies naked,
Clothed only in the
Shreds of dignity
Woven by the love
Of those who care.